Lemon!

Lemon!

sixty heroic automotive failures

TONY DAVIS

THUNDER'S MOUTH PRESS
NEW YORK

LEMON!
SIXTY HEROIC AUTOMOTIVE FAILURES

Published by
Thunder's Mouth Press
An Imprint of Avalon Publishing Group Inc.
245 West 17th St., 11th Floor
New York, NY 10011

AVALON
publishing group incorporated

About the Author

Tony Davis has written about cars for twenty years on and off. He has driven some of the fastest, most expensive, and most impressive vehicles ever built, yet retains a bizarre fascination with those at the other end of the spectrum, those created by designers and engineers who, as he puts it, "think a tour de force is a bicycle race."

Contents

Introduction

Worst Things First!

Most cars are fundamentally good. They look inoffensive, they go well, they are safe, reliable, and durable. And they sell in respectable numbers, returning an acceptable profit to the company that built them. Boring or what?

Lemons, however, are a different thing entirely. Few things in the world provide such a fascinating window into human daring and individuality. After all, there's really only one way to make a good car—with talented people doing things sensibly—but there are a million ways to produce a bad one. And no two car companies stuff things up in quite the same way.

The possibilities are almost endless: you can start with a bad idea, but execute it adequately (the Volvo 760); you can start with an adequate idea, but execute it badly (the Triumph Stag). Perhaps most interestingly of all, you can start with a ludicrous notion and, from there, take the wrong path at every fork along the bumpy road.

Perhaps the best example in this extreme and exalted category is the Zeta, from the South Australian washing machine manufacturer Lightburn. Although the brochure boasted that the Zeta was handsome, the photo made the opposite immediately obvious. And although the gushing spiel blurted on and on *and on and on* about a vehicle that cleverly combined the benefits of a family sedan, station wagon, and van, you could just sense there was something the brochure writer wasn't telling us. Indeed, why did one of the pictures show delivery men loading boxes through the front passenger door?

Closer inspection revealed the truth: although the Zeta looked for all the world like a wagon (a remarkably ugly one at that), some bizarre financial or engineering considerations had precluded Lightburn from providing a rear hatch. To gain access to the cargo area of this ghastly little box of bolts, you had to remove the seats.

There are many marks of a lemon, including catastrophic sales (Ford Capri), dastardly unreliability (Jensen-Healey), bombastic styling (Hyundai SLV), terrifying flimsiness (Goggomobil Dart), uncalled-for longevity (the Fullbore Mark X), and all of the above (Trabant P601). The "build it and they shall come" mindset is typified by the Triumph Mayflower (they didn't come); being left alone at the outermost end of a styling trend is best shown by the doorstop-profiled, knife-edged Lagonda V-8 Saloon. With its 262C, Volvo took an ordinary car and turned it into something unreservedly stupid, while NSU used the Wankel-powered Ro80 to demonstrate what happens when a company confuses its ambitions with its abilities.

As for weird science, what about the Fascination, first with its "boilerless steam engine," and then its "Electro-Magnetic Association" power plant? This, indeed, was a case of concentrated lemon: the Fascination was ugly, daft, and, finally, spectacularly unsuccessful. Not only did it have two preposterously hyped alternative energy sources, but neither of them seems to have actually propelled a car under its own steam, or static electricity.

Other lemon traits include unrealized promise (Rover SD1), deathly dullness (Nissan Pintara), and the corporate hybrid, which cleverly captures the worst aspects of two different brands and combines them in one model. Look no further than that curious Alfa Romeo–Nissan effort called Arna, which smoothly blended Nissan flair and Alfa quality.

The Ford Pinto extended the concept of internal combustion beyond the engine. The De Lorean built its lemon credentials on a solid base of hype, second-rate engineering, and a consistent ability to turn out Monday-morning quality at any time of any day. To this were added stunning hubris, dodgy financial dealings, lousy sales, and a magnificent corporate collapse. Yes, the De Lorean was a car with something for every aficionado of failure.

Readers of this book will find plenty of stupid names—the Daihatsu Naked and the Cony Guppy immediately spring to mind—not to mention the model that has achieved the highest citrical accolade: it has become a byword for getting it wrong. Drive on down, Ford Edsel.

There are those who defend the Edsel. Edsel clubs are now found across the United States, despite (or, more likely, because of) this model's unutterable ugliness. Yet for all the flaws, the Edsel and indeed the Leyland P76, Gaia Deltoid, Lightburn Zeta, Moller Skycar, and others herein are truly heroic failures, products of companies that were prepared to go out and have a red-hot go at changing the rules. Cars that are just not very good can never really compete.

I should mention too that it is hard for me to cover so many different lemons without varying the language a bit and resorting to the occasional Aussie expression. Hopefully the context will make things pretty clear. The only word that completely flummoxed my editor was "donk"—which somehow derived from "donkey"—and is a popular term for engine. It's not a negative term. Donks can be good or bad, though in this book, expect the latter.

That brings me to one last point: one man's lemon is another man's peach. Some readers will dispute my inclusions, others will decry my omissions. But enough of all that—now it's time to hit the track. Gentlemen, start your lemons. Okay, try again. Is the battery charged? Maybe it's flooded. What was that crunching noise?

Lemon!

Ford Edsel

Failure by Another Name

When Ford set up a completely new division in 1955, a snappy name was needed. Extensive surveys were undertaken and over 20,000 names submitted. Learned panels considered designations such as Resilient Bullet and Varsity Stroke, while market research companies studied public reaction to such extravagant monikers as Andante con Moto and Utopian Turtletop.

Having undertaken all this groundbreaking polling, Ford executives proceeded to totally ignore it, deciding instead to use the name of the late son of the equally late Henry Ford I. Unfortunately, his name was Edsel.

Edsel was a quiet and sometimes brilliant man whom Henry had bullied, humiliated, and—some Ford family members thought—hurried to an early grave. If his name had positive connotations in Detroit, it did little to inspire the rest of the U.S.A.

The Edsel's stylist, Roy Brown, was determined to give the new model a bold, upright grille instead of Detroit's usual horizontal treatment. His early clay models were quite stylish (in a 1950s context), but by the time every Ford executive demanded a change here or there, and every accountant found another place to trim a few cents, the eventual result was anything but.

Ridiculously overhyped throughout its development period ("the first truly new car from a Detroit manufacturer in twenty years"), the Edsel turned out to be little more than a hybrid of existing Ford and Mercury models, with new styling and a few extra gimmicks, such as a steering wheel–mounted push-button automatic gear selector and a speedometer that flashed when a preset speed was reached. The grille inset was popularly described as a "horse collar," but Ford people preferred the term "impact ring." They claimed the central bump in the hood directly above it was a safety feature, giving owners "a sense of direction."

In August 1957 the Edsel was unveiled to an estimated 53 million Americans during a Bing Crosby–Frank Sinatra live TV spectacular. Four versions were available—the Ranger, Corsair, Pacer, and Citation—with a choice of two V-8s: a 361 and a 410. If the Ford-generated hype on TV, in the print media, and outside every dealership across the United States wasn't enough, there was also a song:

> *We want our friends to understand*
> *When they observe our car*
> *That we're as smart and successful and grand*
> *As we like to think we are.*

The combination of the newcomer's familiar body and shockingly unfamiliar grille left one commentator to describe the Edsel as "a Mercury pushing a toilet seat." Even more memorable was *Time* magazine's description: "an Oldsmobile sucking a lemon." Despite these comments, most of the initial media was positive (further proof that, like successes, failures become more glorious with time). *Popular Science*, for example, declared, "The Edsel—to use a horse-breeding term—is by Jaguar out of Alfa Romeo."

It also gushed about "more engine power than the average motorist will know what to do with, gadgets beyond a gadgeteer's dreams of glory," plus "styling that reverses the years-long trend to horizontal-pattern front ends, and chrome enough to tax the output of the world's mines."

However, the projected sales of 200,000 vehicles per year proved optimistic by a factor of more than three (the actual total for year one was a dismal 63,110). In 1959—when the grille was redesigned

to look like a plain old horizontal Detroit job—the sales reached just 45,000, and Henry Ford II announced the whole division was for the bullet. By then Ford had released its new Falcon, a compact car that was on its way to setting new sales records.

The Edsel had lasted just two years and two months, and some estimates suggest Ford tore up $250 million on it. The frontal styling was certainly one problem, the dismal build quality another. Equally important, the car was too expensive, a problem compounded by an economic slump. Buyers were looking for smaller, cheaper cars such as the VW Beetle, the very trend that led Detroit to develop compacts such as the Falcon. By the 1960s "edsel" had become a popular byword for lemon. The *Webster's Unabridged Dictionary* made it official.

De Lorean DMC-12

Back to the Maker

John Zachary De Lorean was, by all reports, a real charmer. The bejeweled playboy certainly impressed General Motors, which made him head of its Pontiac division. Then "GM's youngest-ever vice president" leaped even higher. He became boss of Chevrolet and convinced almost everyone within earshot that GM's lavish presidential office was his for the taking. It was not to be. In 1973 De Lorean suddenly resigned, mumbling something about "pursuing a dream."

Some suggest he was pushed. Either way, John Z put his name to a bitter book called *On a Clear Day (You Can See General Motors)* and set up his own company to build "an ethical car." Unlike most dreamers, De Lorean eventually got his automobile company up and running. Unfortunately, however, the ethics his car reflected were his own, rather than those of the broader community.

To get the project off the ground, De Lorean had to first convince

a few important people their money was safest in his care. The socialist British government was as unlikely a source of cash as any. Next thing, our man was sitting on $156 million of British taxpayers' money on the condition he made his U.S.-bound cars in Northern Ireland.

Soon a plant popped up in Dunmurry (near Belfast) and John Z. attempted to show a couple of thousand inexperienced workers how to turn out gull-wing-doored, stainless-steel-bodied, rear-engined V-6 sports cars from scratch at a proposed rate of 20,000 per annum. That the fine folk of Dunmurry weren't very successful at this wasn't really their fault. The design, penned years earlier by Giorgio Giugiaro, was underdeveloped, and production schedules were founded on blue-sky optimism.

Lotus's founder, Colin Chapman, was brought in to solve the manifest problems, but he proved far more interested in helping John Z. pocket the British government loans, grants, and special subsidies than in straightening out the production line.

The build quality of the De Lorean DMC-12, released in mid-1981, was woeful. Furthermore, the design was tail-heavy and noisy and expensive to build and slow. Visibility was poor, the gull-wing doors were a disaster, and the stainless-steel bodywork found few friends.

Sales were calamitous. Those customers who had been found wanted their money back, and within a year the De Lorean Motor Company was put in the hands of a bankruptcy administrator. By then it was discovered that over $20 million of research money had been diverted to dodgy bank accounts in Switzerland and Panama.

In October 1982 the British administrator announced the final failure of rescue attempts. Within hours John Z. was arrested for trafficking 220 pounds of cocaine, an indiscretion allegedly undertaken to raise $50 million to keep the company afloat. Meanwhile, as the legal net closed tighter, Colin Chapman succumbed to a fatal heart attack (or disappeared, if you believe the conspiracy theorists). De Lorean managed to beat the drug charges but the defense was entrapment—rather than, for example, "I didn't do it."

Around 8,500 De Loreans were made (records are contradictory). In the mid-1980s the film *Back to the Future* made the DMC-12 famous for the second time. The film made money.
John De Lorean died in March 2005.

Packard Predictor

American nomenclatural know-how gave us such majestic handles as Eliminator, Mach 1, Turnpike Cruiser, Super Motion, and Packard's very own Predictor. This stunningly . . . something machine was first displayed at the 1956 Chicago Motor Show and can possibly be linked to the demise of the Packard Motor Car Company soon after. It was a demise that the Predictor failed to predict.

Around 1954 the Packard company had made the decision to buy Studebaker, a daft idea that looked likely to guarantee that neither brand would last long. By 1956 Packard was already on the decline, having built only 10,000 cars for the year, compared with 116,000 in 1949. Being further weighed down by Studebaker's exceedingly inefficient manufacturing operations didn't help. The Packard-Studebaker concern was bought by Curtis-Wright Corporation just after the Predictor was shown, but the Packard brand dribbled to a stop circa 1958. The new owners managed to pick up and

drag Studebaker into the 1960s, but the brand finally ran out of steam in 1966.

The Predictor featured hidden headlights and a grille that made the nose of the slightly later Edsel look almost understated. Added to this were dogleg windshield pillars, a Ford Anglia–style reverse-rake roof, opera windows (each with a chrome flash through the center), fins with high-mounted aerials, and triangular taillights. The sliding roof panels were said to aid entry; with the benefit of hindsight they could possibly be considered a forerunner to the detachable-panel "targa" roof. Then again, why give these people any credit?

Triumph Stag

A Lavish Flaw Show

When an owner stands by his Triumph Stag, it's usually because he can't get the door open. Yet there was a time when the Stag seemed to represent an exciting future for sports cars. The styling was well received. The technical specifications (including independent rear suspension) and luxury features also impressed, while the two-plus-two seating lent a degree of practicality not usually found in open sports cars.

Most impressively, the clever T-bar roof seemed to get around new 1970s safety legislation that appeared destined to outlaw convertibles. But in the end, the convertible luxury Triumph was famous only for being famously unreliable, and its optimistic early buyers were soon thoroughly Stagmatized.

The newcomer was based on a stunning 1965 show car by Michelotti, but Triumph—by now a division of British Leyland—was somehow deluded into thinking a stylish body could lift its image and allow it to compete with Mercedes and the like. If delusions of grandeur were not enough, the Stag was designed in a hurry, engineered on a shoestring, put together with nothing even approaching care, and backed by an imploding Leyland.

Launched in the UK in July 1970 to a good media response and strong back orders, the Stag soon became just another British Leyland horror story. It cost the company millions in warranty claims, and millions more were spent in the frantic but ultimately unsuc-

cessful attempt to fix the inherent design problems as production continued.

For a mystifying reason, the engineers had decided against using the lightweight alloy block Rover V-8 engine, which in various forms would power a wide range of British Leyland vehicles, including the Range Rover and the Leyland P76. They may have decided it wasn't unreliable enough to wear Triumph nameplates; either way, they opted to join two Triumph Dolomite four-cylinder engines via a common crankshaft to create a unique, and uniquely horrible, 3-liter V-8. Chronic overheating often led to major engine damage. If that didn't get you, timing-chain failure would. Or the crankshaft bearings, or . . . you get the picture. And for all that, the homemade V-8 produced only 145 bhp (109 kW), leaving the long, narrow, and fairly heavy (3,170 pounds) Stag chronically short of breath.

The Stag's price was high at the start and nearly doubled within a few years. Still, by 1975 there were 16,500 examples on UK roads. Or pulled over at the side with the hood up. About 7,700 had been exported by that time, too. Most went to the U.S. where the car was launched in 1971 and discontinued by popular demand just seventeen months later.

Standard equipment ran to electric windows, power steering, and wood-grained dash. Although the Stag had four seats, the rear was a kids-only zone, and the downside of the clever T-bar construction was high wind noise. Amazingly, this became even louder when the optional removable hardtop was fitted. This ludicrously heavy hardtop was best installed or removed with the help of a football team, yet it invariably leaked.

The Stag Mark II of 1973 brought a blacked-out tail panel and blacked-out door sills, which wasn't exactly addressing the sharp end of the problem. But despite a fast-deteriorating reputation, the Stag staggered on until June 1977. In his book *Making Money from Collectable Cars* (Marque Publishing, 1988), Cliff Chambers put it very succinctly: "As an investment, the Stag is best ignored, since maintenance costs will exceed any profits you may make. But if you are a mechanical masochist, this is your car."

Daihatsu Naked

In 1998 Daihatsu decided there was a niche for a car aimed at buyers who wanted the Schwarzenegger-tough look of a Hummer, the American military vehicle, but were actually hobbits.

The slab-sided automotive midget that resulted was called the Naked. Yes, you heard correctly—Naked. Why? Perhaps somebody had already registered the name Stupid.

Forward motion came from a 660 cc (40-cubic-inch) twin-turbo engine, while other features included a "relocatable instrument panel" and "detachable multi-air folding rear seats." No, I don't have a clue either. Maybe we should check with some-

one who is less than three feet tall and has hairy feet . . .

According to the Japanese marketing guff, the Naked was "so basic, it's advanced," and the company president, Iichi Shingu, described it as a vehicle "that could only have been created by Daihatsu." This comment met with little disagreement.

Lagonda V-8 Saloon

Shock Wedge

There are few British brands with a history as checkered as Lagonda, founded in Britain in 1906 by a sewing-machine engineer from Ohio. And few brands of any origin have built anything as outrageous as the Lagonda V-8 Saloon.

The compressed background is this: the Lagonda won the 1935 Le Mans 24-hour race while the company staved off financial ruin for the umpteenth time. In 1947, after a few more close encounters with the official bankruptcy administrator, the company was purchased by the David Brown tractor group, which already owned Aston Martin (another brand that was no stranger to financial problems). Lagonda cars ceased production in the early 1960s, but the brand was reactivated in 1976 for this, the V-8 Saloon.

The styling was the work of William Towns—the man responsible for various Aston Martin models, including the DB-S coupe—and the

steel body, its wedge shape reminiscent of a door stop, was dropped onto the extended chassis of an Aston Martin two-door. The 5.3-liter V-8, for the most part hand-built, produced in the region of 332.5 bhp (250 kW), thanks to four twin-throated Webers, and squished out its power through a Chrysler Torqueflite automatic transmission. To this point it all sounds like fairly normal Aston Martin fare, an impression reinforced by the presence of lots of dead cow and felled trees in the interior. But take a quick look and a deep breath . . .

The *Star Trek*–like interior was intended to be as futuristic as the door-stop exterior. There was an over-the-top single-spoke steering wheel, soft-touch switches and an LED digital instrument panel that, with the common sense of hindsight, looks like the display from one of those build-it-yourself digital watches sold by electronic stores of that era.

For a brief period the reborn Lagonda was heralded as "the world's dearest [most expensive] . . . saloon." It was certainly a more accurate tag than "the world's best." More than anything, the Lagonda V-8 Saloon represented a bargain-basement attempt to use existing mechanical components in a body envelope that afforded almost no room for such things as engine ancillaries and exhaust plumbing. All the bits (most borrowed from the high-hooded Aston models) needed to be shoehorned, rerouted, and generally crammed under that daftly flat and low nose. Reliability problems were legion.

The English magazine *Autocar* called it "the world's only four-door two-plus-two," a reference to the almost complete lack of space afforded the rear passengers. Lagonda's wedge was also a shocker to park, on account of the long, low snout. And it was not much more fun to drive quickly, thanks to overly soft suspension. Performance was more leisurely than power figures might suggest, though this was a luxury saloon, the makers reminded us, not a sports coupe. If speed was the primary consideration, an Aston Martin coupe or convertible was available.

Rarely has a piece of futuristic design dated so quickly. Yet ironically, the wedge sold better than its Aston coupe cousins produced at the same Newport Pagnell headquarters, thanks to it being a favorite of sorts in the Middle East.

The Lagonda V-8 Saloon had been launched at £25,000; a decade later it went for an almost unbelievable £75,000. Amazingly, it stumbled on until 1990. By then the overly square design cues had been rounded, the interior had been redone, and the mechanical bugs, if not completely squashed, certainly had received a good hit on the head with a shoe. The suspension had also been tweaked and the car was at last heralded as a good thing to drive. But the best thing about driving it remained the fact that you couldn't see it from behind the wheel.

More than 600 V-8 Saloons were eventually produced. However, the Aston Martin–Lagonda outfit continued to be a serial offender when it came to going broke, being bought out and going broke again. It was finally put out of its misery when Ford grabbed it in 1987, becoming the sixth owner in fifteen years.

Ford Nucleon

It was in 1958 that Ford unveiled a car that took advantage of the latest, greatest alternative fuel source: nuclear power. The Nucleon, displayed at American motor shows as a scale model rather than a full-size "concept," was claimed to be capable of traveling 4,800 miles without refueling.

The strange placement of the wheels was said to be due to the huge weight of the reactor. One could expect that after more than a few minutes in the can-tilevered front seat, the Nucleon owner would get sea-sickness—and perhaps a migraine in the second head growing out of the middle of his chest. Sample morning radio traffic report: "The state of California was evacuated this morning after a two-Nucleon collision."

Subaru 360

The Sub-Veedub

The late 1950s and early 1960s brought a flood of Japanese microcars. These included the Mazda 360, the Suzulight 360, and the Mitsubishi 500, each a reminder that before Japan made cars that were reliable, well-built, and stylish, they made cars that were un-, badly, and less than.

The forerunner of the Japanese minis, though, was the Subaru 360, created when someone at Fuji Heavy Industries discovered that Japan's "micro-vehicle" legislation—created to make motorcycles and three-wheeled delivery vans affordable—could be adapted for cars.

The Subaru 360 appeared in March 1958. It was a radical four-wheeler that sneakily complied with all the micro laws by having an overall length less than 9.9 feet (shorter than the original Mini-Minor), a weight below 771 pounds, and a sub-360-cc (22-cubic-inch) engine. Buyers could use a cheaper restricted driving license and pay about one-tenth the road tax of those buying a full-size vehicle.

The Subaru 360 was designed to be just big enough to carry a family of four while offering all-weather protection. Instrumentation consisted solely of a speedometer, the turn signals were manually operated blinkers and the four-speed transmission lacked proper synchromesh. The doors were of the forward-opening "suicide" type, the body a mishmash of poorly fitting panels, while the bottom of the rear wheels tucked in under the tail to make sure the finished product never looked quite secure in the upright position. But the 360 was cheap.

Many considered the Subaru a shrunken VW Beetle. They certainly had in common an air-cooled, rear-mounted engine, rack-and-pinion steering and fully independent suspension using torsion bars on all wheels. However, the Subaru had only two cylinders and its microscopic engine—a two-stroke with a built-in propensity for overheating and seizing—screamed its head off to produce just 16 bhp (11.5 kW). Although the maximum speed was claimed as 50 mph, the handling was so dodgy it is unlikely anyone was game enough to try it.

With its 10-inch wheels, the Subaru managed to scoop the Mini-Minor's least commendable feature. The Subaru's wheels could disappear into things larger vehicles didn't even consider to be potholes.

FHI used the name Subaru (rather than Rabbit, the name of its scooters), taking it from the Japanese term for the cluster of six stars otherwise known as the constellation Taurus. It managed to build just

604 vehicles in the first year, but convertible and light-commercial derivatives joined the lineup as production improved. Subaru also offered a 423cc (26 cubic-inch) engine in export markets.

In the United States the paths of Subaru and an entrepreneur named Malcolm Bricklin crossed in the late sixties in a fashion as colorful and ill-fated as one would expect from the man who would later give his name to one of the world's truly incompetent sports cars. Bricklin first imported Rabbit scooters into the States, then formed Subaru of America and marketed the Subaru 360 sedan under the unlikely slogan "Cheap and ugly does it." By U.S. standards, the Subaru 360 was so small it should have been labeled "Not for individual sale." Yet Bricklin discovered that the car's tininess exempted it from U.S. emission and safety regulations. It was a much-needed exemption.

The timing was interesting, for if you were to create a list of everything that Americans were looking for in a car in 1968, the Subaru would have lined up perfectly with the "not required" column. To Americans the VW was already minuscule—a scale replica of it made no sense at all. *Road & Track* magazine stated that the Subaru was "of uncommon ugliness" before recording a dismally slow 0-to-50 mph acceleration time of 36 seconds (the road testers were aiming for 60 mph, but the car wouldn't make it).

Bricklin made a song and dance of the frugal fuel use, but that was an advantage almost anywhere but the United States, where fuel was so cheap that Oldsmobile and others happily marketed cars with engines 20 times the size of the Subaru's. The American lack of interest in the 360 became even more pronounced when *Consumer Reports* magazine labeled it "the most unsafe car in America."

With Subaru's six stars in freefall and 1,000 unsold cars in stock, Bricklin started FasTrack International, a franchise operation aiming to offer dollar-per-lap car-racing theme parks. Each franchise came with 10 Subaru 360s, presumably to remind budding racing drivers that motor sport is dangerous. When FasTrack achieved all the success it deserved, Bricklin slid out of the whole operation and embarked on the path to losing millions of other people's dollars building a "gull-wing" sports car bearing his own name.

Meanwhile, there were happier things in store for Subaru. And for all its faults, the little Subaru stayed in production until 1970. By then, one million had been sold, mostly in Japan.

Panther 6

More Is Less

It was in England in 1972 that Panther Westwinds Ltd. commenced business—if selling cars at a financial loss can be called a business. As well as blending a Rolls-Royce and Triumph Dolomite in its strange and unnecessary Rio model, Panther made an even odder contribution to the motoring world of the 1970s.

It was a sports machine known as the 6, on account of it having 50 percent more wheels than most people expected when they bought a car. The idea of a six-wheel road car wasn't entirely new. A few cross-country vehicles had been built with an extra set of wheels, just in case. But the Panther was certainly the first sports car thus equipped; its extra wheels were said to be there for improved on-road acceleration, braking, and handling.

The downside of the unusual layout was that it cost more and nobody really needed it. But that seemed a small consideration when you saw how much press was generated by the announcement of this vehicle.

The idea was already proven, up to a point, by the Tyrrell racing team, which had won a Grand Prix the previous year with a six-wheel Formula One car. Tyrrell used conventional wheels at the rear, but tiny wheels on the front, reducing the height—and therefore the aerodynamic drag—of the front end. It also put more rubber on the road for greater cornering grip.

The Panther 6 of 1977, however, used almost the same-size wheels on the front as the back and was thus burdened with many of the disadvantages of having six-wheels—extra weight, complexity, and rolling resistance—without a profile that afforded a really low ground-hugging nose. And, to house a 7.9-liter Cadillac V-8 with twin turbochargers, the Panther 6 had the longest tail in the automotive kingdom.

Between the long nose and even longer tail was a tiny two-seater cockpit nestled behind a vast windshield. The instruments were digital and there was a television and phone, plenty of leather and suede, and very little elbow room.

The overall styling treatment brought to mind Lady Penelope's car in the original *Thunderbirds* television series. The quoted price was a then-monstrous £40,000 but it was said that 15 orders were taken at the British Motor Fair of 1977. A year later Robert Jankel, the company's owner (pictured on p. 24), seemed no closer to fulfilling orders for the Panther 6, so he arranged for some car magazines to have supervised access to the car, presumably in the hope that this would convince the doubters. Jankel first explained to the road testers that the production delays were due to Pirelli not supplying the right tires, so some special allowances had to be made for the handling idiosyncrasies—proper suspension calibration could only be done with the final tires, he said.

Under the heading "Is it a bird? Is it a plane? Is it a joke?" *The Motor*, a British magazine, took to the wheel and—having identified various unusual handling tendencies on a straight stretch –threw the Panther 6 into a corner. "Certainly the sheer adhesion of all that rubber is tremendous," they concluded, "but at high cornering speeds you are very much aware of the huge mass of engine behind you, threatening to swing the tail out like a massive pendulum."

The magazine's test driver also found the steering uncommunicative, the brakes lacking, and the acceleration from rest less than expected of such an enormous engine; they also detected a tendency for the front tires to "tramline," or follow grooves in the road. Yet the journalist still walked away seemingly of the opinion that some new tires and a tune-up of the carburetor would calm the savage beast. "There is some fine honing to be done [but] it works, it's for real, and it's beautifully made," was the remarkably soft conclusion. Panther never had the chance to prove the case. Series production never eventuated, supposedly because of the problem with obtaining tires. Rather than buyers. By 1980 the company was in receivership.

Urbanina

A cross between a motor scooter and a car, the Urbanina was conceived by a group of Italian designers from Pisa and unveiled at the 1965 Turin motor show. Supposedly slated for volume production, this so-called "traffic beater" had a 175 cc (10.6-cubic-inch), 8.5 bhp (6.4 kW) engine, two seats, and excellent headroom. That said, the female in the motor show press photos—possibly the very person immortalized in the song "The Girl from Urbanina"—seemed to be having trouble controlling the vehicle while stationary. Have pity on her and other road users if it really were to reach the claimed top speed of 60 mph.

Daimler SP250

Strange Fish

With a heritage dating to the 1890s, the Daimler company had worked hard to shape its reputation as a maker of staid, solid, luxurious conveyances. And it maintained that reputation right up until 1959 when the venerable British company's corporate brain fell out and it decided to release the SP250.

The first and only sports car to wear a Daimler logo wasn't just any old roadster. It was the oddest-looking one in the sports-car world, with bug eyes sticking out of a strangely curved nose and a radiator grille that looked like the mouth of some form of bottom-feeding marine life.

The slab sides were broken up by oddly protruding wheel arches and there was a step in the profile to make way for fins that didn't so much as blend in as blend out. But there was one thing uglier than an SP250 with the top down: an SP250 with its tall, square, ill-fitting canvas roof in the "up" position.

Aimed squarely at the U.S. market, which was then grabbing every British sports car it could get its hands on, Daimler's roadster was launched as the Dart at the 1959 New York Motor Show. Chrysler had registered the name Dart and demanded that the Daimler name be withdrawn. It could have performed a bigger service for humanity by demanding that the whole car be withdrawn.

"Breathtaking as its performance is Dart's styling!" boasted the original brochure. "From sleek, fluted grill to flaunting rear fins, every eye-appealing curve of its polyester body expresses the spirit of speed."

The copy would have served better to deceive if it hadn't been placed directly under an illustration of those allegedly eye-appealing curves. Still, the newcomer had disc brakes, which was unusual, and a homegrown V-8 engine, which for a British car was even more so. This 2.54-liter overhead-camshaft unit was developed from a "V Twin" Triumph motorcycle engine. Despite this—and the fact it was originally meant to be air-cooled (leading to an under-the-hood

spaghetti of cooling hoses on early versions)—the V-8 worked surprisingly well and spat out a healthy 140 bhp (105 kW). The problem was the car around it.

The SP250 exhibited atrocious wobbling and shuddering because of a lack of body rigidity. Britain's *Autocar* magazine noted that the driver's door tended to pop open during hard cornering. The omission of bumpers as standard equipment was curious, while handling was average at best and extremely dependent on the right tire pressures. Top speed, though, was a shade under 120 mph—an impressive figure helped along by the lightness of the polyester body. Which, presumably, never needed ironing.

By the way, the English company was called Daimler because in 1893 Frederick Simms negotiated to build German Daimler vehicles under license in Britain. In 1926, the original German company, Daimler Motoren-Gesellschaft (formed by Gottlieb Daimler in Cannstatt, near Stuttgart, in 1890) merged with the company started by Karl Benz to become Daimler-Benz. Benz's company had already established the name Mercedes, so the Mercedes-Benz name was used for cars from the merged company. The British firm, dubbed the Daimler Motor Company in 1896, stuck with the Daimler name.

For Britain's Daimler, the SP250 ended up not so much an exciting sports adventure as a death throe. In 1960 the company was swallowed by Jaguar. As Jaguar was in the process of preparing its E-Type model for market it had little need for a fish as strange as the SP250. However, orders had been received from American dealers, so a decision was taken to proceed with production of the Daimler SP250 and hope for the best.

The best did not happen. The U.S. market may have been grabbing every British sports car available, but it was prepared to make an exception in this case. After about a year, Jaguar engineers heavily reinforced the SP250's plastic body to stop its scuttle shake. Bumpers became standard equipment. However, the body reinforcement didn't eliminate cracking panels, drooping doors, and other problems. What wasn't polyester still had a tendency to rust. And what didn't rust remained unspeakably ugly.

Only 1,200 SP250s were sold in left-hand-drive markets, including to Americans, for whose tastes the styling had supposedly been created. The grand total of all sales, before production officially spluttered to a halt in 1964, was a miserable 2,645 units.

Jaguar XJS

Sour Puss

Beware any vehicle that people defend with the phrase "Yes, but it has lots of character." When those fateful words are uttered you know it's a Jaguar or an Alfa Romeo that is being discussed and some poor owner is throwing buckets of money into a black hole with the misguided notion that they are taking part in a "special experience."

Look no further than the Jaguar XJS coupe. If an elephant is a greyhound designed by a committee, then an XJS is, similarly, a sports car suffering from far too much conciliation and arbitration. In an attempt to upset no one, and in effect pleasing exactly the same number of people, Jaguar ignored the golden rule of sports-car building: it has to come from the heart.

The looks weren't the worst thing about this mid-1970s indiscretion. With the XJS, Jaguar almost perfectly combined the comfort of a sports car with the agility of a limousine.

The XJS was impressive in a straight line, certainly, but only when the insanely complicated, notoriously thirsty V-12 engine was working. Jaguars of the mid-1970s to mid-1980s were so unreliable that many Jaguar dealers made 80 percent of their profits out the back door. Which is a way of saying that four out of every five dollars coming into the dealership were for spare parts and repairs.

The starting point for the XJS was the legendary E-Type Jaguar. This had been launched in 1961 to rave reviews and, even if it had become fat and outdated in its lifetime, it remained a more interesting car than its replacement. What wasn't known at the time of the changeover was that cost pressures would mean that this replacement would need to stay on sale for 20 years, forcing Jaguar to enter the multimedia age with the automotive equivalent of a valve radio.

This writer recently found some notes from the last new XJS he tested, circa 1992: "seat doesn't go far enough back, no room next to the brake pedal, forced to curl left foot around the brake pedal . . . sore after 20 minutes of driving. Excessive wind-noise at 35 mph [this was the steel-roofed version!]. Bodywork covered in ill-fitting, overlapping chrome moldings. Steers like a speedboat; weighs a massive 4,100 pounds and feels it. Carpet slid away underfoot, to reveal a mess of wires, rough felt and assorted plastic pieces."

The list went on. And so did the XJS, not getting a well-warranted bullet behind the ear until 1996.

Triumph Mayflower

More an Adversity than a Triumph, the Mayflower was a ludicrous attempt to graft the bodywork and associated grandeur of a large and powerful British limousine onto a small and powerless Triumph chassis.

Introduced in 1949, the Triumph Mayflower acquired nicknames such as "the watch-charm Rolls-Royce," plus many things less kind. The vehicle and the oppor-

tunistic name were apparently created to appeal to Americans. It was assumed they held English limousines in high regard and therefore would go for the same thing in a concentrate.

Unfortunately, nobody asked the Americans what they thought before production commenced, and Triumph ended up shipping only a few more Mayflowers to the New World than the Pilgrims had in 1620. The company came to its senses in 1953 and abolished the model, then wrote it out of most official corporate histories.

Mini Moke

Exposed!

Like some missing link between the vintage and modern automobile (or the skateboard and soapbox racer, if you want to be particularly cruel) is the box-sided, doorless, windowless Mini Moke. The Moke story—the name came from a slang word for donkey or inferior horse—started in the late 1950s, when the British Motor Corporation (BMC) answered the call for a light vehicle for the UK Army.

Unfortunately, BMC's answer wasn't the one the military was looking for. The boys in green rather selfishly demanded good ground clearance, easy maintenance, and go-anywhere performance. The Moke couldn't offer the first, with its tiny (10-inch) wheels, fell down on the second count, with its complex Mini-Minor power train, and failed on the third due to front-wheel drive. In an attempt to give the vehicle some measure of Jeep capability while preserving the compact size (after all, the Moke was designed to be stacked flat in aircraft cargo holds), some experimental four-wheel-drive versions were built. One had an engine and transmission at each end—a sort of bodiless, push-me-pull-you Mini.

By 1963 the army had rejected every variation BMC could come up with, so it was decided to make a civilian version. This went on sale in 1964 with two-wheel drive and (just one) 850 cc (52 cubic-inch) engine. It was motoring at its most basic, with a punt-style chassis made from steel pressings, and pannier-style boxes along each side to give rigidity and house the battery, fuel tank, and tool kit. Not surprisingly, the lack of body work proved a problem in the British Isles weather and buyers stayed away in record numbers. It

was then that BMC, in accordance with English tradition, sent the unwanted to the colonies.

Moke production was transferred to Australia in 1966, where the vehicle quickly became known as the Mini Joke. In standard form, only two seats were fitted and there was no rollover protection. Weather protection, meanwhile, amounted to a fold-away (and often blow-away) fabric roof. As well as being cold and wet for much of the year, Moke drivers had to endure Mini-Minor reliability without even getting Mini weather protection or a lockable trunk.

At least the Moke was cheap, for much of its life bearing the mantle of the least expensive four-wheeled road vehicle on the Australian market. Out in the bush, the Moke was expected to find a ready market among farmers who couldn't afford Land Rovers. The hitch proved to be the relative lack of power and low ground clearance, which combined to make it an almost useless workhorse. In 1968, BMC Australia offered optional 13-inch wheels, a year later a 1.1-liter engine was fitted. This turned the Moke's fortunes around . . . er, 360 degrees.

The Moke's failure as a working vehicle led to a refocusing of its image as a fun recreational vehicle ("Things go better with Moke," cried one ad) and, alternatively, the ultimate thrift machine ("Moking is not a wealth hazard," cried another). By the early 1970s a new version known as the Californian was on sale, complete with paisley vinyl soft-top, lurid body colors, improved seats, and a 1,275 cc (77.5 cubic-inch) engine. Further upgrades were made through the 1970s.

In 1976 a Danish-born adventurer, Hans Tholstrup, used his

Moke–rubber dinghy hybrid to cross the notoriously rough Bass Strait between Tasmania and the Australian mainland. Such stunts were not enough to save the Moke, though; it never achieved a 2CV-style cult following, though there are now a few clubs around the world, including North America.

Production of Australian Mokes ceased in 1981, after a total of 26,142 had been built for local and overseas markets. That's a miserable average of 1,600 per year, but the story didn't end there. Production was again transferred, this time to Portugal, where Mokes were built until 1992. The tooling was then sold to the Italian company Cagiva, which produced a further 1,500 or so in Portugal then shipped the tooling to Italy. And there lies the Moke's main claim to fame: very few cars in history have stayed in continuous production for 30 years without ever being a success.

Tucker 48

Damned Torpedo

The Tucker 48 appears in some lists of the Greatest Cars Ever Built, and the man behind this late 1940s streamliner—a Michigan-born former car salesman named Preston Thomas Tucker—is the subject of the idolatrous film *Tucker: The Man and his Dream*, directed by no less a figure than Francis Ford Coppola.

The true believers will tell you that Mr. T was visionary, his car, revolutionary; the whole venture, a noble attempt to break Detroit's thoroughly evil GM-Ford-Chrysler cartel. This retelling suggests that the Tucker car was festooned with technological and safety features that major makers had conspired to suppress, and that even the government was in on the plot to bring the upstart company down. In this David and Goliath battle, Goliath was not only bigger, he was the one with the slingshot.

The case for the prosecution paints Preston Tucker as a shady character who wasted and even misappropriated most of the millions he raised from mom-and-pop investors. His project, they argue, was so fanciful the Big Three would not have lost even a moment's sleep over it, let alone hatch a major plot to stop it.

The story started in 1946, when Preston Tucker unveiled a sketch of his "Torpedo," and produced a lot of fast talk about how this was a "car of the future for the everyday man" and had already been the subject of 15 years of development. It was a good time to sell a dream; with the war over and a scarcity of new cars even from the major carmakers, there was plenty of pent-up demand and blue-sky optimism. Investors and potential dealers lined up to throw their money—a remarkable $26 million of it—at this tall and charming man in a sharp suit. Tucker also persuaded the War Assets Administration to do him a winning deal on a massive factory in Chicago.

The Torpedo prototype, now called the Tucker 48, was unveiled amid great showmanship in July 1947. However, beneath the glitz and gloss the prototype was a hurriedly thrown-together effort to placate increasingly nervous investors and the Securities and Exchange Commission (SEC), which had begun taking a keen interest in Tucker's business maneuvers.

Using Tucker's instructions, the designer Alex Tremulis drew up the body and produced something that looked slightly ahead of Detroit's mainstream efforts but was hardly the leap into the distant future promised by the early sketches. One notable feature was a center headlight that turned with the wheels.

Despite Tucker's claims that it was "the first completely new car in 50 years," the prototype's transmission had been salvaged from

HOW FIFTEEN YEARS OF TESTING PRODUCED
The First Completely New Car in Fifty Years

Tucker '48

a prewar Cord and its body fabricated around a 1942 Oldsmobile. The SEC would soon argue that the Tucker operation had neither the expertise nor the serious intention to turn this hand-built one-off into a series production car.

The prototype also lacked many of the safety features Tucker had earlier boasted about such as disc brakes and seat belts. Of those that were present, the so-called crash padding on the dash was of dubious value and the provision of an area into which the front-seat passenger could duck before a collision was just plain silly.

As for the mechanical layout, what worked for the Volkswagen Beetle became the stuff of low comedy when what you hung over the back axle was a huge "six" with a capacity of 589 cubic inches, or 9.65 liters. This massively heavy but not overly powerful engine needed two truck batteries to turn it over. If such a tail-heavy machine wasn't going to go around corners very happily—even with the smaller 335-cubic-inch (5.5-liter) donk that replaced the original 589—the Tucker should at least have been good in a straight line. The later engine was designed for a helicopter and supposedly produced 165 bhp (123 kW), compared with the Chevy six's 90 bhp (67 kW). On the other hand, the Tucker weighed more than 2 tons and the power output figures were as suspect as Tucker's claimed "130 mph top speed" and "35 miles per gallon" fuel economy.

A pilot production run of 50 cars was pushed through to convince investors and the SEC, which stepped up its investigations when Mr. T raised yet more money with an advance purchase plan on Tucker 48 accessories. These 50 cars were hand-built at monumental expense, yet the price was a bargain $2,450. In 1948 Tucker published an open letter outlining his woes. His factory, he wrote, was infiltrated with industrial spies and he was being undermined by competitors with friends "in high places in Washington." He suggested elsewhere that other carmakers were bullying their suppliers into withholding parts. In reality, Tucker was years away from being in a position to order parts in serious quantities. It is also likely that Tucker's advertised price would put him in the red at least as quickly as any skullduggery from competitors.

Tucker and his associates went to trial on 31 charges of fraud but were eventually found not guilty. It was little consolation, because by then the Tucker concern was thoroughly bankrupt. In 1951 the man at the center of it all did what any man in his circumstances would—he flew to Brazil to seek financial backing for another new car, this time a sports model called Carioca. This project still hadn't come to fruition when Tucker died of cancer in 1956, at the age of 53.

Fullbore Mark X

Look familiar? Contempt-breedingly so? Perhaps that's because the Fullbore Mark X of the 1990s was merely an updated and re-Anglicized version of the Hindustan Ambassador, a model that had been built in Calcutta since 1959 and was itself based on the Morris Oxford.

By the time it was again sold in England, the Morris/Hindustan/Fullbore was fitted with an Indian-assembled 1.8-liter Isuzu engine, plus such delights as drum brakes all round (with no power assistance) and what was described as Foot-o-Matic windscreen wipers. What the "matic" bit referred to is unclear—you cleared the screen with a very manual thump of your left foot.

The London-based importing company Fullbore Motors promoted the Mark X as a robust, no-nonsense car that one could comfortably drive while wearing a hat. "The Fullbore Mark X is a fine compromise between the charm of the 1950s and the mechanical strength and build quality of the 1990s," said a spokesman, perhaps getting it the wrong way around.

To give at least a hint of the second decade referred to in this rather optimistic assessment, the car was repainted and retrimmed when it hit the Southampton docks. There, such niceties as seat belts, mirrors, a catalytic converter, and chrome hubcaps were added, and all liquid was drained from the cooling system and washer bottles for fear of bringing in waterborne diseases. Despite all this effort, the Fullbore company seems to have fallen off the map around 1998.

Leyland P76

The End of an Error

In many ways the Leyland P76 was a good car. But, alas, in many more ways it was a bad one. The all-new big family car of 1973 was meant to save an already sick Leyland Australia, but it sold poorly, made an inglorious exit only 15 months after launch, and took the rest of the company down the drain with it. Along the way it established a reputation as Australia's Edsel—and with good reason.

So what was good? The P76 was a big, comfortable family car with the option of an interesting alloy block 4.4-liter V-8 engine, a donk developed from the Rover 3.5, in turn developed from a General Motors V-8. The car boasted an aerodynamic wedge-shaped body, some advanced-for-the-day engineering features and—*drumroll, drumroll*—a trunk large enough to accommodate a 44-gallon drum.

And what was bad? Where to start? The slogan was "Anything but Average," which proved to be sadly true. Every car seemed to have

Leyland P76. Anything but average.

a unique combination of faults. The model number P76 came from the engineer's project number, itself arrived at when the Leyland supremo, Lord Stokes, read the code "P76" from the back of his watch during a business meeting. It may have been more helpful, however, had Stokes taken note of some of the other terms on the back of his watch—such as "dust-proof" and "water-resistant."

Even if people accepted the P76 shape (which was not popular) and could live with its gargantuan size, they still had to put up with any combination of the following: rust, internal drafts blowing in from huge gaps in the panels and poor seals, myriad squeaks and leaks, smoldering carpets (due to a poorly insulated exhaust system), interior fittings that shook loose, fast-deteriorating paint, and the choice between a six-cylinder engine that was an underper-

former or the alloy V-8 that went hard but was prone to overheat in traffic and in some cases to corrode internally. There were also windshields and side windows with an unnerving ability to come unstuck on rough roads, or even under heavy braking.

The joke was that when you delivered a P76 for work under a warranty, it was quicker to tell the mechanic the things that *didn't* need fixing. The car became popularly known as the P38—only half the car it was supposed to be—but the problems were bigger than the car itself. Leyland was a hostage to bad management, hostile

unions, national industrial policy that constantly changed without forewarning or apparent awareness of consequences, severe budgetary problems, poor production design, and dud components from supplier companies experiencing similar problems as Leyland itself. Worst of all, the company had launched the P76, a big car, during an energy crisis, a "premium" price model in a time of severe inflation and deteriorating consumer confidence. And they had courageously done it all under a new badge, Leyland, rather than using Austin, Morris, or another handle familiar to Australians.

Despite all this, the V-8 version won Australia's *Wheels* magazine Car of the Year award for 1973. The decision has embarrassed the magazine ever since but, to be completely fair, the call was made before all the quality glitches were apparent, and at a time when only locally built cars were eligible for the award. This made the field rather narrow. So narrow, in fact, that something built by Leyland Australia during the 1970s could win.

Sales failed to pick up and a "Force 7" coupe variant, complete with a novel hatchback rear door, was frantically readied for market in the desperate belief that it could help save the farm. If Leyland Australia had survived, the Force 7 would have hit the market in 1975, by which time sales of big coupes had collapsed and the Aussie arms of GM, Ford, and Chrysler were preparing to phase out their Monaro, Falcon hardtop, and Charger two-doors, respectively. Leyland—which had managed to lose around Aus$71 million (which was then just over $100 million American) in an era when a new family car cost less than Aus$4,000—had maintained its disastrous timing to the end.

Bristol Blenheim

Old Bomber

You may be able to forgive a four-speed transmission, solid rear axle, pushrod engine, separate chassis, and general dearth of modern technology in a twenty-first-century car if it is extremely cheap or looks drop-dead gorgeous. But what about when it costs a fortune and looks like a 1970s Ford Capri coupe suffering from water retention?

That's the question one has to ask when confronted with the Bristol Blenheim, a conveyance still in production in the new century and priced as we go to press at something exceeding £140,000. Yes, do not adjust your book. That price was £140,000, or nearly $270,000.

The Bristol Blenheim takes its first name from the city in which it is built and its second from a World War II fighter-bomber from the days when Bristol was a major aviation manufacturer. Which was a very long time ago. After World War II, with something of a slump in aircraft demand, Bristol took the same route as Messerschmitt and others: it turned to cars. To ease the transformation, Bristol bought licenses from BMW and produced its own versions of these German cars in the United Kingdom.

Bristol Cars had some success at Le Mans in the early 1950s, and since the very early 1960s the brand has been under the guidance of a former race-car driver named Tony Crook. The 1960s and 1970s brought a series of Chrysler-engined cars, some with aviation-themed names such as Beaufighter and Brigand. The Blenheim coupe's flat-sided, oddly proportioned shape goes back to the Bristol 603 model of the mid-1970s, though it seems the name Blenheim wasn't used until the 1990s.

The official production estimate for the Blenheim is "no more than 150 per year," though an independent estimate puts it perhaps more realistically at "around two." No outsiders are allowed to visit

the factory where the cars are banged together—sorry, hand-crafted—because the workers are supposedly also involved in secret design work for the aviation industry. It is to be hoped that this work is a little more up to date than anything they are doing with road vehicles.

But back to the appearance of the Blenheim car. The official literature avoids terms such as "porky piece of 1970s excess," preferring the more reassuring affirmation that the appearance "is carefully tailored to achieve quiet understatement yet maintain an elegant, timeless line." It also says the Blenheim—the product, it adds, of the only luxury-car maker under British control—takes three to four times as much labor to build as other luxury cars and is a "true gentleman's Grand Touring coupe favored by the most skilled and enthusiastic drivers."

"In a Bristol," we are told, "every journey becomes an occasion, a relaxing and satisfying place from which to observe the hectic world without."

Inside are the usual British luxury accoutrements, including soft leather seats, thick carpets, and slabs of walnut veneer, though assembled with 1960s and 1970s construction techniques and design sensibilities. To save cost the Blenheim incorporates many off-the-shelf components such as Vauxhall rear-light clusters, while beneath that 1970s body is pure 1950s technology. There's a huge separate chassis under a hand-beaten aluminum skin. This soft and expensive aluminum doesn't result in particularly lightweight, though. The Blenheim weighs nearly 2 tons, despite being a comparatively modest 16.5 feet long.

The engine, a 5.9-liter V-8 borrowed from Chrysler, is also ye olde worlde. A four-speed auto box is standard, and a dual-fuel engine (gas and liquefied petroleum gas, or LPG) was offered circa 2003 to reduce running costs and improve emissions.

Electronics? Not many. Bristol claims its own mechanical brake assist system, say, gets along very well without the need for any fancy-shmancy computer-controlled antilock overrides. A stability control system? Yeah, sure. It's called the steering wheel.

The claimed performance is 0-to-60 mph in a sprightly 6.3 seconds, but this and claims of outstanding aerodynamics, stupendous refinement, and stunning performance have been hard to verify, since members of the press are not given access to evaluation vehicles. Well, they might give away secrets to Jerry, old boy.

Davis

The Boot Scooter

It looked like a full-size dodge-'em car. Or perhaps a shoe. It had three wheels, and although claimed as a four-seater, all the passenger seats were arranged in a straight line across one padded bench.

It was to be built by an entirely new company in California (not exactly the heart of the U.S. motor industry) and powered by a Hercules engine normally used for stationary applications, such as roving military spotlights. Stability was questionable, and a weird quirk of the suspension system meant the nose actually rose during heavy braking.

But there was madness in the methods. And fraud, too. Behind the ballyhooed "world's biggest three-wheeler" was one Gary Davis, born in Indiana in 1904. During the 1920s and 1930s Davis worked as a used-car salesman while building an impressive collection of ex-wives, creditors, and disgruntled business partners. Shortly after

World War II, Davis decided to build his own car. One of Davis's claims was that the legendary screen actress Greta Garbo was among his financiers. If a lie, it was an ingenious one, as silent partners couldn't have come much more silent than Garbo. As for the car itself, the origins appear to lie with Frank Kurtis, a racing engineer, who built a three-wheel roadster with a V-8 engine circa 1940. This represented a complete departure from the usual idea that a three-wheeled layout was the domain of underpowered economy cars.

After a scam that enabled Davis to acquire Kurtis's three-wheeler for $50, the vehicle was modified and renamed. Davis's head engineer, Peter Westburg, later described his boss as a "quick talker with a ready grin that made you feel at ease. He could borrow the shirt off your back and sell it back to you and you would swear that you had gotten a bargain."

The unveiling, in 1947, of the oddly curved aluminum-bodied Davis car—to sell for a bargain-basement $995—came with huge razzle-dazzle. In a series of road shows across the United States in 1947 and 1948 the public was transfixed by such innovations (or gimmicks) as hidden headlights and built-in hydraulic jacks that could raise the body automatically when a tire needed changing. Indeed, in some places the Davis created almost as much excitement as the bigger, flashier Tucker of the same era.

When people questioned the stability of such a large three-wheeler, Davis paid a Hollywood stunt driver to attempt to turn the car over, apparently without success. Celebrities such as the actor Red Skelton were drafted into the promotional effort, and commission agents, it seems, were taking orders with deposits almost as soon as the prototype was displayed. Hundreds of people also signed on as dealers, which raised as much as $1.2 million.

The Davis was a grab bag of borrowed parts. Many things changed from one car to the next; one early prototype seems to have had a V-8 (like the car it was based on), another a six-cylinder, but most were powered by the front-mounted four-cylinder Hercules, which drove the rear wheels. No matter which engine was fitted, however, Davis's claim of "100 mph and 50 mpg" was nonsense of the utter variety.

Many people believe that Preston Tucker, for all his shortcomings, intended to build and sell his controversial Tucker 48. Fewer believe Davis had any such plans for his car. There was plenty of money coming in but little evidence that it was being spent on the things needed to meet the proposed production schedule of 50 cars per day in 1947, ramping up to 100 a day in 1948. The things Davis did spend company money on, according to court records, included a Beverly Hills home for himself, mink coats for acquaintances, and various other items not entirely necessary for volume automotive production. And by one account none of Davis's workers ever received paychecks for their efforts.

By 1948, those who had purchased dealer franchises were screaming for cars that never seemed to arrive, and legal authorities were trying to unravel the highly creative corporate structure that had been created. They succeeded, and in 1949, with just 17 Davis cars built, the man with his name on the bodywork was finally hauled off to jail for fraud and the carmaking operation was wound up. Davis was released after two years and died in 1973.

Ford Capri

Open Season

It should have been so good. It brought together proven Mazda mechanical components, a swag of top designers, highly skilled engineers, and the promise of the first affordable convertible sports car since the MGB died of old age and neglect, in 1980. Yes, it should have been a Mazda MX-5. Alas, it was only a Ford Capri.

Where to begin? Back in the 1980s Mazda and its partial parent, Ford, were simultaneously working on small four-cylinder roadsters. Although it was obvious to all that Mazda's Japanese-built MX-5 had the edge in styling and superior handling, insiders didn't see it as serious competition for Ford. Ford would have its roadster out first and the Capri had one thing that Mazda had no answer for. Information on exactly what this one thing was has since been lost, but we do know that Ford pushed ahead, even though there were so many delays that Mazda beat it to the mar-

ket and signed up most of the potential buyers of a light convertible sports car.

The Capri—styled in Italy, screwed together in Australia, powered
by a Mazda four from Japan, and taking its name from a defunct
British Ford model—was developed in Melbourne specifically for the
American market. Unfortunately, the Ford Motor Company decided to
use the little roadster as bait to get younger punters into its fune-
real Lincoln-Mercury dealerships. Ford Australia's main chance was
merely the American Ford company's novel experiment. Which failed.

Not that everything could be blamed on the recipients. The Capri was underdeveloped, rather dodgy in the quality department, and hard to get excited about. And the styling was questionable. The taillights looked like they were upside down, the interior was pure budget hatchback, and the slab-sided wedge body was more 1970s than 1990s.

People will forgive a sports car many sins if it's pretty. If not, it's got to be very quick. Here Ford missed out again. Even in its turbo form, the Capri felt less sporty than its Mazda competitor, and Ford's two-plus-two seat configuration (versus Mazda's two seats only) and bigger trunk were not enough to make the difference. With the MX-5, lowering the roof was a simple chuck over the shoulder. With the Capri, you almost needed to call for roadside assistance. Then there was the scuttle shake, plus a generous selection of rattles, squeaks, leaks, and design failures. Many of these were fixed with the Series II. But it was too late.

By being pretty and having its act together from day one, the MX-5 sold strongly and scooped just about every "car of the year" award around the world. At one stage it seemed people were inventing awards just to give them to the Mazda MX-5. By contrast, Ford Australia struggled from day one. The company needed sales of 25,000 cars a year to make its Capri project viable. The figure was almost reached in the first year, with nearly 20,000 sales in the States and 4,000 in Australia. After that, the Capri didn't come close. There was no choice but to bring the curtain down.

Hyundai SLV

From the moment it was unveiled at the 1997 Seoul Motor Show, Hyundai's SLV concept car divided observers. There were those who didn't like it, and those who absolutely despised it.

Nobody, however, failed to notice the Korean "Super Luxury Vehicle," with its Picasso-with-a-hangover styling and monstrous exterior dimensions (18.5 feet long and roughly halfway between "too wide" and "much too wide"). Hyundai's official line was that the SLV's fiber-reinforced polymer body was "eye-catching," but an executive from a rival brand, Daewoo, got a lot more mileage with the line "It looks like the car Scrooge McDuck uses to take his money to the bank."

The car was so unpopular with motor-show crowds that its builder avoided the usual tease line of "this concept car is a good indication of the styling of our exciting new models to come." Instead, Hyundai's supremo, Mr. B. J. Park, carefully explained to anyone who would listen that the company had "no intention of developing a production model that looks anything like the SLV."

Volvo 262C

Anyone for Squash?

Throughout the 1970s Volvo was flying a holding pattern. It developed its box-on-a-box 140 series into the equally boxy 240 series and then killed off its weird-as-all-get-up-but-fondly-remembered P1800 coupe (as driven by Roger Moore in the original British television series of *The Saint*).

The company's image was slipping in every market, while economic factors were making the once-affordable "Swedish taxis" far too expensive. Against this background, the company's president, P. G. Gyllenhammer, commanded his designers to produce something really special, something that would revitalize Volvo's luxury image and create unprecedented excitement for the brand. Gyllenhammer, a genuinely messianic speaker, no doubt delivered this request in something akin to a Swedish rendition of the hugely stirring St. Crispin's Day speech in Shakespeare's *Henry V*. And spurred on by this rousing, poetic call to arms, what did Volvo's finest produce? The 262C.

The Volvo 262C was just about the dumbest coupe derivative ever built. Even though it had completely unique bodywork turned out at vast expense by the Italian autobody builder and design house Bertone, it looked for all the world like an everyday Volvo sedan that had been hit by a lift. In *Car and Driver*, journalist Rich Ceppos pointed out that at $16,000, the 262C cost two grand more than a Cadillac Eldorado. He added "if you're a normal-sized adult, an ability to magically shrink your torso is what's needed to fit inside without hitting your head."

In Australia *Wheels* magazine summed things up when it called the stratospherically priced coupe "The Car for Little People with Big Wallets." Rival *Motor Manual* reported that a bystander had asked its road tester, "Who squashed ya car, mate?"

The daftly low roofline that defined the car was not a clever optical illusion. It was achieved entirely at the expense of headroom. About 2.5 inches disappeared, along with a great deal of rear visibility. Mechanically, the newcomer was standard Volvo 260 series: rear-wheel drive, front engine. It used the shared Renault-Peugeot-Volvo 2.6-liter OHC V-6, a dull performer that gave Volvo sixes of the day a slower 0-to-60 mph acceleration time than their cheaper four-cylinder stablemates.

The 262C's interior had all the required luxury items (lots of dead tree and cow, and plenty of electric assistance), while the bodywork carried Volvo and Bertone badges plus what looked like a funny swirly crown. This was the crest of the king of Sweden, who apparently was a great fan of the design. And evidently no basketball champion.

There were various theories about the reasons for the 262C's dubious styling. The most convincing was that the designers at Volvo just didn't have a bloody clue. Consider the statement made at the time of the car's launch by Volvo's chief designer, Jan Wilksgaard: "The 262C brings out the underlying sporty elegance that Volvo has always perceived as their image and expresses it more clearly. It's a very personal car that makes a statement."

Buyers made their own statement: "You must be joking."

Lightburn Zeta

Fifteen Minutes of Shame

"It's a family sedan! It's a station wagon! It's a delivery wagon." So blared the advertisements in 1963 for "a new conception in motoring," a vehicle its manufacturers heralded as "the culmination of ten years of research and more than one million miles of road testing." Called Zeta, it was made "for the world" by South Australia's Lightburn Industries, better known for its washing machines, concrete mixers, wheelbarrows, and car jacks.

This "new conception in motoring" looked suspiciously like a big box on tiny wheels and had the sort of bug eyes you'd find in a dark corner of the fish market. What's more, the roofline clearly reflected the washing-machine lineage.

But if one look at the Zeta doesn't tell you why it was a showroom wallflower, consider its practical attributes. For one thing, you had to stop the engine and restart it to engage reverse. And the

IT'S A FAMILY SEDAN!

IT'S A STATION WAGON!

IT'S A DELIVERY VEHICLE!

COMPARE ZETA'S FEATURES

• *Impact resisting, rust-proof fibreglass body. *All-round independent suspension. *Powerful Girling hydraulic brakes. *Michelin tyres. *Flashing turn indicators. *Scrubbable upholstery and interior trim. *Economical, almost maintenance-free two-stroke engine with "Electramatic" reverse.*

Zeta

BY LIGHTBURN

A LOW-COST RUNABOUT DESIGNED FOR BUSINESS AND PLEASURE

Zeta combines versatility with extreme simplicity of design and rugged engineering, to bring you a new concept of economical personal or business transport.

The compact engine-gearbox-differential unit drives through the front wheels to give you and Zeta a straight through flat floor and the largest USEABLE interior space of any comparable small vehicle! As a family sedan Zeta seats two adults and two or three children in foam cushioned comfort.

Wide doors swing through 180° and all seats can be removed in seconds to allow easy loading and stowage of bulky packages. On fishing or surfing trips, two six foot adults can sleep on Zeta's flat floor in easy comfort! Extremely simple controls and sparkling performance makes Zeta a delight to drive in heavy city traffic or on the open road — prove it yourself with a test-drive now!

ZETA SUCCESSFULLY COMPLETES 1000 MILE NON-STOP PROVING RUN IN 22 HRS. 25 MINS.!

In February 1964, a standard Zeta covered 1000 miles non-stop, between Newcastle, N.S.W. and Adelaide, S.A. It completed the run at an average speed of 44.4 m.p.h., returned 41.5 m.p.g. (50-60 m.p.g. under normal conditions), had absolutely no mechanical breakdowns! This is proof positive of Zeta's rugged engineering and outstanding reliability!

A NEW CONCEPT OF VERSATILE AND ECONOMICAL TRANSPORT

F2121

body? Although it was vaguely wagon-shaped, there was no rear door or hatch. You had to get the passengers out and remove the seats to load it.

If the air-duct on the hood suggested speed and power, this was entirely accidental. Forward motion was unwillingly provided by a Villiers two-stroke twin with a capacity of less than a third of a liter. The output was in the region of 16 bhp (12 kW), and this found its way to the front wheels via a motorcycle transmission and chain. *Wheels* magazine said of the Zeta, "Its performance is virtually nil."

To back up, you turned the engine off and engaged an "Electramatic" system that spun the restarted motor in the opposite direction. This gave you a full set of reverse gears and, in theory, the same top speed in either direction.

The Zeta's body was fiberglass and sat on a steel chassis. The interior was large but unremittingly sparse. The "monkey-up-the-stick" column gearshift was a shocker, the engine a nightmare of noise, vibration, harshness, and smoke. Tackling any reasonable-size hill required a run-up of biblical proportions. And road holding? Not very much of it at all. The fact the seats came out was advertised as a practical virtue but was really a necessity to access the cargo area. And on and on the list went.

The head of Lightburn Industries, Harold Lightburn, assured the press that the Zeta had been designed "not only for Australian sales but for an intensive drive on export markets." In, say 1958, the case for the Zeta would have been a tiny bit easier to support. But from 1959, the Mini-Minor had changed everyone's ideas about how good a small car could be. Another telling fact: the Zeta cost £595

in Australia, but a Mini, complete with a trunk lid and conventional reverse gear, cost only £158 more. It was no contest.

Lightburn ceased car production in 1965, having produced just 343 Zetas. That was a long way short of the 50 a week predicted, but 343 more than the Zeta deserved.

Mercifully few, if any, made it into the wider world at the time, though a handful have left Australia in recent years for museums in the United States and Britain.

Chevrolet Corvair

The Roll Model

In the 1965 book *Unsafe at Any Speed*, Ralph Nader, a Harvard Law School graduate, set out to paint General Motors as a corporation with a greater interest in profits than in the safety of its customers.

There was no better illustration, Nader asserted, than the rear-engined Chevrolet Corvair, which, he said, had a flawed, penny-pinching suspension system that caused drivers to lose control during turns and flip the car over.

GM responded in what it considered a sensible, practical, and reasonable way. It hired private detectives to follow Nader in the hope of proving he was homosexual.

But why did GM produce such an unlikely compact car in the first place? In a strange sort of way, its beginnings lie in Germany before the war, because the unanticipated success of the VW Beetle in the United States during the 1950s convinced Chevrolet it needed a lighter car in its armory. And if an air-cooled, horizontally opposed engine in the tail could work for the Germans, why not for the Americans?

Being Chevrolet, it was decided that bigger was better, even if the Corvair was originally envisaged as a light car. So it ended up with a six-cylinder engine in the tail, albeit with a comparatively modest capacity (for the States) of 140 cubic inches, or 2.3 liters. As well as being larger than the Beetle, the Corvair was a great deal more modern, with a monocoque, or unitary body (in which the body is integral with the chassis), and aluminum engine. From a company better known for tarting up old designs with new bodywork than reengineering from the ground up, this was extraordinary stuff.

The first Corvair, released in late 1959, broke other Detroit trends besides that toward larger, heavily decorated cars, with an austere interior, and bodywork unadorned with fins or fields of chrome. It was offered as a two- or four-door. A van, station wagon, and curious "Rampside pickup" soon followed, then a convertible and a pioneering turbocharged engine option.

Nader's allegations concentrated on these early Corvairs of 1960 to 1963, which he described as "the one-car accident." The Corvair certainly had a tendency to oversteer, or hang its tail out. Enthusiasts loved this, but it was not ideal for those who didn't adjust their driving style (most American cars tended to plow forward into a corner with huge understeer), or were lax about maintaining correct tire pressures.

By the time Nader attacked, there were 103 Corvair lawsuits

against GM, and Chevrolet had modified the suspension to control the rear "tuck in" that *Unsafe at Any Speed* blamed for unpredictable handling. But the Ford Mustang was released in 1964 and did more to kill the Corvair than Nader ever could. It offered a powerful V-8, and with fuel being so cheap, who cared about the Corvair's greater fuel economy or mechanical sophistication?

A svelte new Corvair body for 1965 was not enough to tackle Mustang, while the notorious and bungled Nader surveillance operation failed to rid GM of its "consumer advocate" problem. GM's president, James Roche, was forced to apologize to Nader before a Senate subcommittee, and the company eventually handed over $425,000 for invasion of privacy. (It wasn't only homosexuality GM was looking for; evidence tendered showed it would have been equally happy to prove Nader was a Communist or secret beneficiary of Corvair lawsuits).

Like any good zealot, Nader used his newfound wealth to dig even deeper into the automotive industry—and the meat industry

and almost every other potential infringer of consumer rights. In 1966, as a direct result of the Corvair affair, the federal government announced its first National Traffic and Motor Vehicle Safety Act.

It is widely believed Chevrolet would have dropped the Corvair in 1967 for commercial reasons, but didn't want to be seen to be running. So the Corvair stumbled on until 1969, recording sales of just 6,000 in its final year, compared with nearly 330,000 in 1961. Buyers of the last examples needed to be coaxed with a credit toward the purchase of a future Chevrolet.

Meanwhile, none of the eight Corvair cases that went to trial were successful and the final twist came in 1972, when the National Highway and Traffic Safety Administration finally released its report into Nader's allegations. It concluded: "The handling and stability performance of the 1960–63 Corvair does not result in an abnormal potential for loss of control or rollover, and it is at least as good as the performance of some contemporary vehicles, both foreign and domestic."

Nader considered the report a whitewash. Corvair supporters had the bittersweet comfort of knowing the car had been pardoned after its execution.

Triumph TR7

Bad Sports

The TR7 hit the UK market in late 1974, hailed as the Leyland conglomerate's first genuinely new sports car in a decade and a half. Many other dramatic claims were made for the scallop-sided coupe, but the TR7's only substantial achievement was to make every backyard kit-car maker feel like a fine craftsman.

The TR7 was built by an imploding British Leyland in the industrial nightmare that was 1970s Britain. Even the most sympathetic reviewers struggled to find positive words for the massive bumpers, the huge, heavy tail, and that gruesome crease along the side, but the styling, alas, was the high point.

Britain's *Motor* magazine performed a 12-month 12,000-mile test on one example, and the car only just made it. By the end of the test, the car's drivetrain had been virtually rebuilt under warranty, yet the car still had what the magazine described as "disfiguring rust" and a myriad of other problems. "A particularly nasty lemon" was the magazine's summation.

Triumph designers had aimed the car at the American market at a time when safety and emission regulations were changing drastically. In their attempt to solve a whole lot of new challenges from the bottom floor of the poisonous Leyland bunker, they ended up with a tintop when traditional TR buyers expected a convertible. And they ended up with a strict two-seater at a time when the four-seater ("two-plus-two") version of Datsun's Z-Car was outselling the standard version four to one.

The TR7 was designed to look midengined, but its power plant was in the nose. There were boasts of new aerodynamic benchmarks, but road testers complained of "unbearable" noise at 80 mph. The

TR7's barely adequate power was courtesy of a 2-liter, 92 bhp (69 kW) four-cylinder borrowed from the Triumph Dolomite sedan. There was acceptable handling, to be just, and a five-speed manual transmission. But to the standard Triumph fare of poor ventilation, dodgy controls, unreliable electrics, and dismal build quality, the TR7 added poor outward visibility in all directions, doors that simply didn't fit their openings, and—wait for it—tartan upholstery. Okay, that may not have been strictly speaking a fault. But it was certainly avoidable.

The TR7 went on sale in the United States in 1975, but 18 months later almost a whole year's production was lost to strikes before production was moved from Liverpool to Coventry.

So desperate were the Australian marketers, they ran advertisements showing the TR7 as a double bed on wheels. The caption read: "This is how your girlfriend's mother will view your new TR7." Very daft indeed.

By the end of the 1970s, an open-top TR7 became available in the U.S. and UK. Even a V-8 version (TR8) saw the light of day, but the game was up. Within a few years Triumph would go the way of Alvis, Austin, Morris, Riley, Wolseley, and all those other expired British Motor Corporation/Leyland brands.

FSM 650

Unpolished Pole

Known as the Nikko, Niki, Polski Fiat 126, and FSM 650 during its 27-year run, the automobile that Poles nicknamed Maluch ("the toddler") was the result of a deal between the Polish state and Fiat in the very early 1970s.

The first models—made in Bielsko-Biala, south of Warsaw—rolled off the line in 1973, and they increasingly turned up in Western countries during the 1980s. FSM stood for Fabryka Samochodow Malolitrazowych, which rolled off the tongue as gracefully as this crude, pensioned-off Fiat took to the road.

How the FSM 650 passed Western safety and emission laws into the 1990s was never fully explained. The engine, which hung over the back axle, was a 652 cc (40-cubic-inch), air-cooled, two-cylinder, carbureted screamer with a manual choke that, if not used judicially,

would flood the engine. Flood the engine? What was this? An automobile or a lawn mower?

In the early days you could have any color you liked, as long as it was bleak. It was a peculiarity of the Eastern Bloc that cars were painted in the most drab colors ever devised to guard against inspiring consumerist passion in citizens. However, as exports grew the color choice improved and, supposedly, so did the quality. That leads to the frightening thought of what it was like before they brought it up to "still nowhere near acceptable."

The measuring tape showed the 650's overall length (10.5 feet) made it about 1.5 feet shorter than any other four-wheeler on the market, while its weight of 1,320 pounds was similarly otherworldly (third-worldly, in fact). The engine put out just 24 bhp (18 kW), so to keep up with city traffic you had to bury the right foot and adjust your speed with the gearbox. Gaps in traffic had to be second-guessed in advance, otherwise you weren't going through. Momentum was everything. The noise was indescribable. And, thanks partly to Polish-made Stomil tires, the 650 changed direction like a shopping trolley. Only less precisely.

"This fully imported car has a rear-mounted engine which gives you Porsche-like road holding ability," said one English-language brochure, written by someone who clearly had never driven the 650. In reality, the vehicle demonstrated every handling vice known to suspension engineers, plus some invented especially for this car.

The options list had "not available" next to air conditioning, automatic transmission, and power steering. What you saw was what you got: flipper-style front windows, a single-speed interior fan, drum brakes all round, a non-synchromesh manual transmission. There was not even a glove compartment or radio. The four seats had scarcely enough padding for one. The offset driving position was somewhere between Alfaesque and Kafkaesque. On the plus side, it was very cheap. In Australia, for example, the Aus$7,990 price tag made it exactly $10 cheaper than the leather seat trim option on a Porsche 928.

The 650's speedometer was calibrated to 85, but attempts by Western car magazines to record a 0-to-60 mph acceleration time faltered because the car wouldn't reach the desired speed in the available space. By the time 50 mph came up, over 30 seconds had elapsed. But don't think the lack of power added up to particularly special economy. Indeed, if there was anything to recommend this pocket-size horror, no serious road tester found it.

In Poland, however, the 650 continued to stumble off the production line until the year 2000. By then over 3 million had been made, none of them well.

Pininfarina Diamond Car

Complete with Cadillac-height fins, what looks like a rear roofline from a Citroën Goddess, and a wheel at each of its oddly placed extremes, Pininfarina's Diamond Car was one of the celebrated Italian design house's least celebrated creations. "Diamond" referred, in this case, to the wheel layout.

Built in 1960, it was powered by a rear-mounted 1.1-liter power engine, although information was scant on whether this was supplying power to one, two, three, or four wheels. Advantages of putting the road wheels in places where at least half would miss the tracks on the average garage hoist were claimed to include low torsional stresses, light weight, and reduced production costs.

The idea of a diamond-wheel layout excited almost no serious interest in its day, and has continued to do so ever since.

NSU Ro80

Ro Is Me

Car of the decade. Machine of the future. The most significant automobile since World War II. There seemed no praise too lavish for the stunning new vehicle unveiled in Germany in late 1967.

And some of the acclaim was justified. This front-drive, wedge-shaped exercise in advanced aerodynamics and improved packaging efficiency was truly revolutionary and set the tone for the so-called aero cars of the 1980s. Furthermore, the newcomer was fitted with a Wankel rotary engine, the smooth, compact, and powerful miracle motor that was poised to oust the standard reciprocating engine from its smug position of power.

Yes, the Ro80, built by the German company NSU-Automobil, was one of those cars that comes but once a generation and changes all that follows. The pity was that it sent its manufacturer broke and left tens of thousands of owners enormously unhappy.

The Ro80 power plant had a capacity of 995 cc (60.5 cubic inches), yet developed a comparatively huge 128 bhp (96 kW). That was the good news. The bad went beyond the unfortunate decision to name the engine after its designer, Felix Wankel. NSU was in financial trouble and the Ro80 had been rushed to market before the engineer's considerable concerns about mechanical durability had been fully addressed.

The Wankel proved thirsty, but the main problem was that the engine seals failed to properly seal the chambers created by the tri-angular rotor within the epitrochoidal housing in which it oscillated (you are following this, aren't you?). Engine failure at 10,000 miles or less was common. Around the world, NSU replaced thousands of engines free of charge. But unfortunately they replaced them with Ro80 engines. And the company wasn't completely "mea culpa"; NSU apportioned much of the fault to poor maintenance and "abuse of the free-revving nature of the Wankel engine."

It was a particular shame because the Ro80 had so many virtues. Consider a few: a roomy cabin with a long flat floor, a clever clutchless semiautomatic transmission, a quietness and smoothness that was almost eerie, and a top speed of 175 km/h. There was also excellent steering, brilliant handling, powerful brakes, a standard of fit and finish that drew near universal praise, and styling that, love it or hate it, was as different and distinctive as that of any mainstream newcomer since the Citroën DS of the 1950s (it looks less radical now because, unlike the Citroën, it was widely imitated).

The Ro80 also had such unusual-for-the-1960s things as a heated rear window and a ski hatch in the rear seat. But the car's single most publicized feature—the revolutionary power plant—was its failing. The Ro80 was a great meal brought to the table too quickly. If fitted with a conventional engine, or launched a couple of years later with a better version of the same engine, the NSU Ro80 very likely would have been an enduring success. After all, Mazda was soon to prove that the Wankel could at least be reliable, if never cheap to produce or fuel-efficient.

In late 1969, NSU was financially challenged (okay, bankrupt) and was taken over by VW-Audi. Ro80 production continued for another eight years, while many of the former NSU engineers helped refine and improve the concept for their new employer. Their efforts included the wind-cheating Audi 100CD of 1982. It was this conventionally powered Audi that finally realized the promise of the Ro80.

Goggomobil Dart

Gee, Oh! Gee, Gee, Oh!

The Bruce Weiner Microcar Museum in Madison, Georgia, owns a perfectly preserved Goggomobil Dart, which it describes as "a pretty two-seater in the then-current Lotus idiom."

But as someone who once owned one, I won't hear a nice word said about it. My Goggo, a black Dart with a mind-shattering 16.6 bhp (12.5 kW) lighting up the back wheels (and pulsing, grabbing drum brakes lighting up the front wheels), was bought 25 years after the event. It was in genuine "as-new" condition, which proved to be no benefit.

The story behind this most eccentric vehicle takes us back to the 1950s and a man named Bill Buckle, based in Sydney, Australia. Buckle had previously launched a classy and expensive coupe bearing his own name, but the Goggomobil was at the other extreme. It came after Buckle purchased the local rights to the tiny German

Goggomobil with the intention of marrying imported mechanicals with fiberglass bodies produced Down Under.

The result, launched in 1958, was the smallest and cheapest "family" car on the Aussie market. The two-seater Dart sports variant—conceived and designed by Buckle himself—followed in 1959.

The Dart was only a fraction more than three feet high, and its other statistics were equally oddball. The weight of 748 pounds put it halfway between a motorcycle and a car, which made perfect sense for a vehicle that combined the disadvantages of both.

There were no doors. To help with ingress and egress, the seats rose slightly when you pulled them back. However, the climb over the

sides was not dignified. And you didn't get out of the minuscule Dart so much as flick it off. The original press release said that "safety was a number-one priority." Yet no one in a Dart ever felt even slightly secure. While you looked up at other cars' door handles, the other road users looked straight over you. And if you needed a sudden burst of acceleration, it was best to jump out and run.

The ride was bone-shaking and the steering as light as you'd expect in a such a tiny car. The steering was also billy-cart direct: about one hiccup lock to lock. There was no luggage space and little weather protection (a fold-up roof was optional, but as the Goggomobil had no doors, when up the roof completely trapped the occupants inside). The four-speed motorcycle transmission had the oddest shift pattern in the automotive kingdom and every other Dart feature was on the quirky side of peculiar.

The engine was a two-stroke but felt like less. Placed in the tail, it displaced under a third of a liter (293 milliliters, to be exact), had a 6:1 compression ratio, and developed its maximum speed at what seemed to be about 95,000 rpm. The top speed was about 60 mph, at which point the engine made almost enough noise to drown out the sound of pedestrians laughing as you passed by.

For all that, the Goggomobil had the distinction of being the only independently produced Australian car to make money during the 1950s. Around 5,000 cars were built (most were "family sedan" models but the total also included 700 Darts), before the Mini-Minor arrived in 1961 and totally redefined what was possible in an economy car.

Gaia Deltoid

"Nothing like it" was the slogan for this 1996 three-wheeled British, er, vehicle. Seldom have truer words been spoken. It wasn't just the styling that seemed to have fallen out of a different time-space continuum. The full name was "the Gaia Deltoid Supertrikar" (GDS).

The GDS consisted of a two-seater cockpit with a patent-applied-for "headstock coupling" that allowed a wide variety of motorcycle rear ends to be bolted into the back. The bike's rear wheel was intended to provide all of the go and a third of the stop. Despite incorporating some of the disadvantages of a motorcycle, the tape measure showed the GDS was a very carlike 13 feet long. It weighed not much more than 880 pounds, however, and depending on the bike selected, was said to be quick, very quick, or "warp drive."

Details of exactly what happened to the GDS venture after its bold launch are hard to locate. So are examples of the Supertrikar, although I did find a brochure. It boldly states that the vehicle "draws on the past as much as the future," and provides "echoes of old and new Ferraris and Porsches mingled with the feeling of a racing sports car." That is certainly one interpretation. Another is that it looks like a Mardi Gras float. Just add flight crew.

Rover SD1

Stay Rover, Leak Oil Rover, Play Dead Rover

In the late 1970s, there was no room for shoddy quality within the British Leyland organization. This was because there was already so much shoddy quality within the British Leyland organization they couldn't possibly fit any more in.

Against this rather depressing backdrop came the SD1 from British Leyland's Rover division. It was an innovative design that deserved a lot more. A lot more, for example, than being built by Rover in the 1970s.

The SD1 was first sold in England in 1976 and, like so many British cars of the era, had much to commend it. The big Rover introduced a totally new body concept to the luxury market (it was a hatchback) and had excellent handling. Its styling was bold and strikingly different (not everyone liked it at the time, but the lines have held up remarkably well).

Rover described the five-door as a "midweek gentleman's express which transformed into a weekend family runabout." So popular was the concept that the SD1 secured the European Car of the Year award for 1977, and initial sales on the home market exceeded expectations.

But that, ladies and gentlemen, was as good as it got. Reality was still to be faced and no sooner had Rover built up an order bank than the plant went on strike, drastically cutting supply. Those people who had received cars, however, were not necessarily the lucky ones.

In keeping with BL tradition, it wasn't too long before things started falling off. They were small things at first: switches, wipers, door handles. But then, increasingly, it was the big bits, the ones that made the car stop and go. There was the small matter of

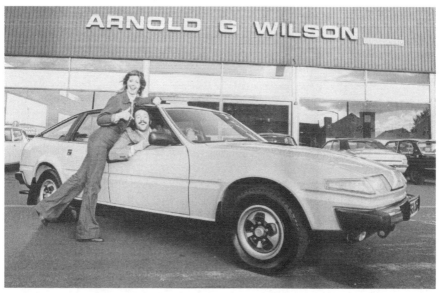

leaks, too, as the rear hatches of the early cars tended to let water in, and the engines and transmissions tended to let oil out. Alas, it was soon obvious that, despite the promising start, this was just another dog called Rover.

Soon after the Euro Car of the Year gong, one English car magazine awarded the SD1 its Worst Car of the Year appellation. A more forgiving journal tested it and reported with apparent satisfaction, "No major disasters, only a few minor trim and equipment failings."

The engine was a 3.5-liter version of the alloy block V-8, originally developed by Buick, that had powered such vehicles as the Leyland P76 and the original, grossly unreliable, Range Rover (and, indeed, later grossly unreliable Range Rovers). The transmission choice was between a pig-heavy manual and a slushy three-speed auto.

The SD1's reputation preceded it, which led to the rather mystifying paragraph in the Australian press release about "a detailed local development and modification programme" and "quality upgrade." The blackened name also ensured that the designation SD1 (it stood for Specialist Division project 1) was not used Down Under, where the model was referred to as the Rover 3500 V-8 and received a whole lot of cheap plumbing to meet local emission regulations.

Not only did the early Australian-delivered Rover 3500 V-8s have fearsome fuel consumption, they took a very leisurely 12 seconds to hit 60 mph from rest. The "executive express" was more of an "executive all stations."

The Rover went through several upgrades, and particularly with the Vanden Plas versions of the early 1980s, it came much closer to realizing its original promise. But by then few people cared and an almost-bankrupt Rover had been forced into a joint venture with Honda. When the Rover SD1/3500 hatch was replaced in 1986, it was by a reskinned Honda Legend.

Alfasud

The Corrode Warrior

It was the car that gave rust a bad name. Even terms such as "gross mechanical unreliability" were reluctant to be mentioned in the same sentence. It was the Alfasud, a mini–Alfa Romeo that was in some ways the world's best small car and in others the most horrible vehicle of any size.

Some of the faults—such as a remote trunk release handle on the passenger side (only slightly closer to the driver than the trunk)—were there by design. Others were specially added during the production process. Many of the things in this second category had nothing to do with carelessness. They were the result of great attention to detail. It was all to do with north-south Italian rivalry.

The background is this: Alfa Romeo traditionally built its cars in Milan, but in the 1960s the company announced a surprise plan to decentralize in a southerly direction. The new plant was to be in

Naples and was to build the lower-cost Alfasud (*sud* being Italian for south) at the unprecedented rate of 1,000 cars a day. The folks in the north didn't take very well to the concept of jobs being sent south. Sabotage might be too severe a word, but the components built in Milan and sent to Naples to be fitted to Alfasuds were bad even by the standards set by Alfa Romeo's northern plant.

To add to this rather fundamental problem, the southern plant had been built in a rush (to meet a target of three years from green field to mass production) and staffed with many people who had never built cars before and didn't appear to be in a hurry to learn. The fruit of all this, er, creative tension was unveiled at the Turin Motor Show in late 1971. The "Sud" was a small four-door sedan with attractive lines and a surprisingly affordable price tag, but the equipment level was sparse enough to preclude carpet, a radio, and any way to prop the trunk lid up (when open, the trunk lid rested on the rear window). Decent ventilation was also off the list. Yet all this and more was forgiven by many road testers once they punted a Sud down a challenging piece of road.

The Alfasud was front-wheel drive, a layout not widely considered sporty. But reviewers enthusiastically (and justifiably) pointed out that the Sud set totally new standards for road manners for a small car. The space efficiency was also excellent, and, providing you didn't mind rowing along the gear lever, the peaky little 1.2-liter "boxer" (or horizontally opposed) engine gave exhilarating performance. However, while the ink was still drying on rave reviews, many customers were seeing their Suds spitting, clunking, and shuddering to a halt. And the biggest problem of all—rust—was yet to appear.

Early Sud glitches went beyond the rattles and squeaks considered to be part of normal Alfa "character." The doors quickly drooped and needed to be slammed. This in turn knocked the flimsy door-mounted side mirrors out of whack. The weather sealing was poor, which exacerbated the corrosion problem, the wind noise was high, the interior door handles fell off, and an Alfasud floor was rarely without a rich covering of small plastic bits that had come from somewhere under the dash or seats.

The high-revving nature of the engine (and, to be fair, the sort of boy racers who bought the car) had a devastating effect. Owners experienced such problems as spark-plug leads that rattled free, carburetors that choked themselves, and throttle cables that jammed, and this was often in the lead-up to more extravagant failures involving enormous mechanical crunching noises and clouds of black smoke. However, rust was the fatal problem. It appeared under the engine bay of many cars within months of delivery and would eventually eat doors, sills, windscreen surrounds, and roofs. The proof is in the vanishing: large numbers of Suds were sold in many countries, but they are very thin on the ground today.

Arbib Dome Car

Styled by the industrial designer and artist Richard Arbib, and built circa 1961 by Andrew Mazzeri, a New York autobody builder, the Arbib Dome Car was presumably thought to be beautiful. And who are we to say otherwise? Ugly bugger, isn't it?

Powered by a four-cylinder engine and made largely of aluminum, the Arbib used an electric motor to raise and lower its glass dome. This prototype was said to have cost the then-massive sum of $35,000. But, for reasons that totally mystify, series production did not follow.

Stutz Blackhawk

A Touch of Crass

The name Stutz seems to spring straight out of the pages of an F. Scott Fitzgerald novel. The revered brand, founded by Harry K. Stutz, had a lineage going right back to the earliest Indianapolis 500 races, and Stutz produced elegant speedsters and sumptuous luxury cars through the 1920s and into the 1930s.

It has even been claimed that the Stutz automobile was such an integral part of the American success story during the 1920s that if anyone committed suicide in one, or otherwise managed to kill themselves behind the wheel, they would automatically rate an obituary in the *New York Times*.

None of this illustrious history, however, has anything to do with an ostentatiously ugly vehicle produced three and a bit decades after the original Stutz company filed for bankruptcy. The story goes that in 1968 James O'Donnell, an investment banker, discovered that Stutz was listed as an "unclaimed corporate name." He wasted no time before making it a claimed corporate name.

Investment banking was obviously treating Mr. O'Donnell well because the offices of the new Stutz Motor Car Company Inc. were in New York's Rockefeller Center, and the famed (rather than, say, tasteful) stylist Virgil Exner was soon engaged to design a new car wearing the famous nameplate. Exner had some experience with exhumations. He had styled a new Duesenberg for a failed 1966 revival of that brand (Duesenberg, like Stutz, never really recovered from the Great Depression).

The new Stutz firm displayed its Blackhawk in 1969, and no one was left without an opinion on the styling. Fake side pipes, trunk lid-mounted spare, faux running boards, two-tone paint, an osten-

tatious grille and outrageous expanses of chrome were all crammed onto a car that was, deep below, a plain old Pontiac Grand Prix. The interior was filled with exotic materials, including fur carpet and outlandishly costly woods and leathers. Buyers received custom-tailored luggage that matched both the interior upholstery and fur-lined trunk.

The standard General Motors V-8 engine was modified to produce a putative (though hard to believe) 400 bhp. The body was hand  assembled in Italy by Carrozzeria Padana of Modena, where 22 coats of hand-rubbed "$100-a-gallon" lacquer were applied. Coupe, convertible, and limousine versions were built, bearing such monikers as Bearcat, Diplomatic Sedan, and Royale Limousine. All were variations of the one design—to get an idea of the scale, consider that those monstrous front and rear overhangs ensured that even the shortest Stutz was around 19.5 feet from nose to tail.

In the States the Stutz price list started at $22,500 and proceeded up the scale to "as much as you'd like to pay." Mink carpet was listed among the accessories. The starting price meant that even the "cheap" versions were among the most expensive cars of the day. To maintain exclusivity even further (as if the styling wasn't enough), the new company charged $8 for its brochures. That was no small amount in 1970.

Elvis Presley, Mohammed Ali, and Sammy Davis Jr.—none of whom were associated with understated tastes—were said to be in the early rush of high-profile purchasers, though one suspects there wasn't exactly an onslaught of others.

By 1971, the (new) Stutz company had changed hands, and neither the new owner nor those who followed seemed to be meticulous record keepers. The most reliable production numbers suggest that about 50 cars were made in the first four years—though, amazingly, the company struggled on through the 1970s and even into the 1980s. A 1976 convertible called the Stutz d'Italia was listed as the most expensive car in the world at $129,000, although the Associated Press noted at the time that "business isn't exactly booming."

By one report the final Stutz was built as late as 1995. For whom, or why, is not clear.

Pegaso

Franco's Ferrari

Spain has never been a high-profile carmaker. For a brief patch in the early 1950s, however, the country threw off its automotive anonymity and produced the spectacular Pegaso, one of the world's most expensive sports cars. The publicity was enormous, the reviews enthusiastic. If there had been buyers as well, it might have changed everything for the Spanish industry.

The background to Spain's brief bathing in the supercar limelight rests with the fascist government of General Francisco Franco and its sudden and mysterious delusions of automotive grandeur. In the wake of World War II (which Spain, battered by its civil conflict of the 1930s, opted out of), most Spanish carmakers produced micros and trikes. These were the only powered vehicles the greater part of the impoverished population could afford. So it was a particular surprise when Empresa Nacional de

Autocamiones SA (ENASA) unveiled the Pegaso coupe at the 1951 Paris Motor Show.

State-owned and known foremost as a builder of buses and trucks, ENASA had centered the unlikely new project around a complex V-8 engine developed by Dr. Wilfredo Ricart, a Spaniard who had previously worked for Alfa Romeo. The first Pegaso, the Z102, was an exquisitely crafted coupe with a 2.5-liter all-alloy quad-cam V-8, Grand Prix–style suspension, and a top speed of 145 mph—in standard form. For those who thought this was too slow, a supercharger was optional.

The Z102 was built with little regard for cost, the government

PEGASO

El coche para el automovilista apasionado

treating the process as "training in excellence" for the ENASA engineers who would soon take on the world. Prices reflected the lavish approach. The most expensive Pegaso was four times the cost of a Mercedes 300SL, itself well beyond the reach of almost any Spaniard.

Within a few years there were 3.2- and 4.7-liter versions of the same 90-degree V-8 engine and no less than six completely different body styles. These bodies were drawn by leading French and Italian design houses but built in Spain. Coupes and convertibles were produced, some boasting understated elegance, others showing ludicrously finned 1950s excess. The premium Pegaso, with supercharged

4.7-liter engine, had a claimed top speed of 160 mph and was heralded as "Europe's most powerful car." By the mid-1950s work began on a Pegaso family saloon, but it never made it to the showrooms.

In 1957 the whole thing ground to a halt for reasons as mysterious as those that had caused production to start in the first place. ENASA went back to commercial vehicle production, having built just 130 Pegasos in six years, and having lost millions of dollars on a fascist folly.

Moller Skycar

Ever since humans have been able to drive and fly, inventors have tried to produce a vehicle that will do both. It's been mostly pie-in-the-sky fantasy, though in 1951 the Aerocar achieved limited success. Never mind that its wings had to be carried in a trailer about as long as a small bus, or that nobody bought it. It could fly, after a fashion, and drive, after another.

Canadian-born Dr. Paul Moller has spent more than 30 years and close to $100 million working on his George Jetson–like, eight-engined, vertical-takeoff Skycar.

He has taken it around the world to talk about (rather than demonstrate) its cloud-hopping, mile-eating capabilities, which he claims include 350-mph cruising with hatchback economy.

Despite decades of hype—the first order was taken in 1974—the Skycar has never flown for more than a minute, and then only on the end of a rope. Still, Moller reckons he'll untether his creation and hit 350 mph soon. At present only one Skycar exists, but Moller says once production hits half a million units a year the price will come down to that of a midsize luxury car. In the meantime the race is on to see which flies first: the pig or the Moller.

Cony Guppy

Small Fry

Generally, the Japanese car industry has managed to keep the emphasis on its successes, which have been many. But there were many early shockers, from the rebuilt English and French cars of the 1950s (from Nissan, Hino, and others) to entirely home-grown atrocities such as the three-wheeled Daihatsu Bee.

One of this writer's favorites—perhaps, I'll confess, because of the altogether ridiculous name—is the Cony Guppy. A product of the early 1960s, the Cony Guppy was the work of the Nagoya-based Aichi Machine Industry Co. Ltd., which had developed from the Aichi Aircraft Co., which, according to a corporate profile from 1961, had been engaged in the manufacture of aircraft for the Japanese Navy "before the war."

As with so many Japanese company chronologies, Aichi's successes "before the war" were followed by more successes "after the war." Strangely though, Aichi seemed to have done nothing in between. By the 1950s it made the decision to try its corporate hand at making automobile components, and then at full-scale car manufacture. Circa 1962 it delivered to an expectant world the Cony range of cars, which included this microscopic trucklet known as the Guppy.

The Guppy brochure came complete with an overlay sheet covered in brightly colored fish. (Both cony and guppy are types of fish,

though they are not found together, since one is saltwater, the other, fresh. Cony is also an Old English word for simpleton—but I digress.) Unusual for early 1960s Japan, the Guppy brochure showed women behind the wheel.

The initial power plant had one cylinder and a thimble-size capacity of 199 milliliters. It developed a claimed 9.3 bhp (7 kW). It was described as four-stroke in some literature, and two-stroke elsewhere. This micromotor was midmounted, leaving the feet of the driver and passenger to hang over the front axle and double as some sort of early warning system for an impending crash. The road wheels looked as though they had been borrowed from a lawn mower, while the front-opening "suicide" doors looked impossibly thin, flimsy, and, well, suicidal.

A delivery van variant with a 360-milliliter engine was sold as the

Cony Giant, a minitruck version followed (the Cony Wide, of course) and there was also a variety of particularly unstable-looking Cony three-wheelers. The three-wheeler didn't seem to have a snappy name, but if the Giant and Wide protocol was followed, it clearly should have been known as the Cony Untippable.

Production of four-wheeled Cony vehicles peaked at about 1,000 a month. In the mid-1960s the Aichi company was absorbed by Nissan, and Cony brand cars went the way of so many other Japanese lost causes. The Aichi Machine Industry Co. name resurfaced again in 1997 when it was announced that the "Nissan affiliate which assembles vehicles, and makes parts at its Nagoya plant" was to spin off its Aichi "electric vehicle department." Unfortunately, little more on the matter was heard and we were never given a name for the supposed Aichi-built electric car. But Cony Guppy was always going to be a hard act to follow.

Cosmic Invader

Carl Casper's battery-powered three-wheeled Cosmic Invader was built in the 1970s (how could you possibly have guessed?) Need we explain why it failed to outsell the Volkswagen Beetle?

Ford Pinto

Passengers Alight Here

The Pinto "subcompact" was named after a horse. A piebald horse. A piebald horse with a tendency, one assumes, to explode.

The Ford that would become known as "the barbecue that seats four" was rushed to market for the 1971 model year as a counter to Chevrolet's equally unexciting but considerably less flammable Vega. At first only a two-door Pinto sedan was offered, but the range was soon expanded to include a Runabout model with a hatch door at the rear, possibly to give easier access for rescue crews.

There was nothing innovative about the Pinto's styling or engineering, but the price was right, the four-cylinder engine was reasonably economical, and sales were strong. But by 1974 Ralph Nader's Center for Auto Safety was demanding a recall, arguing that the Pinto's tendency to concertina in rear-end accidents did more than rip open the badly positioned fuel tank. It tended to jam the doors shut.

As combinations go, this was a rather worrying one, but Ford refused to change a thing, offering the Department of Transportation such inventive arguments as "retooling for the changes would take 43 months" (considerably longer than it had taken to develop the entire car) and—listen up here—"most of those people were already dead from the impact before the fire started." By 1977, however, the growing band of Pintonista rebels had their manifesto. It was a brilliant piece of investigative journalism by Mark Dowie in *Mother Jones* (named for a celebrated nineteenth-century labor leader), the magazine of the Foundation for National Progress.

Using internal Ford documents and hundreds of collision reports, this article (now archived on motherjones.com) detailed how Ford had conducted its own crash tests and was aware of the hazards awaiting those early buyers. Yet, Dowie wrote, Ford refused to modify the Pinto and even rejected as too expensive a one-dollar plastic shield that significantly reduced chances of the exposed fuel

tank being punctured. Ford had a design brief that demanded the car weigh "not an ounce over 2,000 pounds nor cost a cent over $2,000" and was grimly sticking to it.

Dowie wrote that despite as many as 900 deaths in Pinto fires, Henry Ford II continued to vigorously campaign against new safety legislation. "Compliance to these standards will shut down the industry," he said repeatedly. But what made the most impact was *Mother Jones*'s detailing of Ford's now-notorious "cost-benefit analysis." This assigned a value to each fatality of $200,000 and to each serious burning of $67,000 and argued that the cost of fixing the Pinto exceeded the cost of deaths and maimings (when calculated in such a way).

Ford's reluctance to modify was perhaps driven by arrogance, but also by the high cost of new tooling and the fact that a different fuel tank would compromise trunk space (an important selling feature). The Pinto continued to ignite debate—and motorists—and Ford even launched a "woody wagon" version. Sure, its sides were covered with plastic woodgrain rather than real timber, but it still seemed to be adding fuel to the fire.

Ford said the *Mother Jones* article was filled with "distortions and half-truths," but nevertheless recalled 1.5 million Pintos. Shortly after this recall started, cost-benefit analysis calculations were blown to bits when a Californian jury awarded a Pinto victim, Richard Grimshaw, a record $125 million in punitive damages. A year later Indiana prosecutors charged Ford Motor Company executives with reckless homicide.

The Pinto's own funeral pyre was lit in 1980. The Grimshaw judgment was later reduced on appeal (to $3.5 million), the executives were acquitted on the reckless homicide charges, and, strangely, none of the fuss ever greatly hurt Pinto sales. So perhaps Ford was right all along: a low purchase price and a trunk that takes a second set of golf clubs *is* better than a long life and happy retirement.

Riley Elf

After World War II, the British Motor Corporation (BMC) enjoyed a 46-percent share of the British car market and controlled many of the most revered automotive brand names in the history of the Sceptered Isle. Yet it managed to squander both its market share and every single one of the brand values of every single one of those brands. Evidence of how it accomplished this feat is provided by cars such as the Riley Elf.

No points for guessing that this 1961 atrocity was an adaptation of the Mini-Minor, cleverly preserving the cramped interior without maintaining the compact, park-anywhere exterior dimensions. And, in the process, turning the simple and elegant into the ornate and ugly. If the Riley Elf wasn't silly enough, there was a Wolseley Hornet version, too.

Rolls-Royce Camargue

Rolls of Fat

The arrival of a new Rolls-Royce is hardly a common occurrence, yet when 1975 brought that very thing there were more groans than (restrained and dignified) yelps of joy.

Although described as the last word in high tech (which, incidentally, is "tech"), the new Camargue was merely a rebodied R-R Silver Shadow with a bit of extra equipment, including the forerunner to climate-control air conditioning. And it was packaged in an awkward, angular body, styled by Italian design house Pininfarina and looking more like an obese kit-car conversion than a coach-built masterwork.

The Camargue—named after an area in southern France with which the car had no connection whatsoever—was billed as a "two-door fixed-head coupe." This was a subtle way of indicating it had many of the disadvantages of a convertible without any of the pleasures of a roof that could be taken down.

More pointedly, the Camargue reinforced that its builder had reached the end of the familiar road. With the low volumes being achieved by Rolls-Royce in the 1970s and the crimping of the research and development budget that came as a result, the crew from Crewe no longer had any chance of building a better car than Mercedes-Benz and others—particularly when so much of Rolls-Royce's comparatively meager R&D budget now had to be directed toward meeting evermore rigorous government legislation.

Rolls-Royce clearly had to trade on elegance and exclusivity, yet the Camargue brought only the second of these—an exclusivity that was a lot more extreme than planned. Just 534 Carmargues (including eight prototypes and test vehicles) were built over an 11-year period.

The boxy body—hand-crafted by Rolls-Royce's longtime coach builder, Mulliner Park Ward—was a good pointer to that of the forthcoming Silver Spirit sedan, another fatty that once again would repackage the familiar mechanical configuration of a 90-degree-OHV V-8 powering the rear wheels via a three-speed automatic transmission. Maximum speed for the Camargue was listed as 122 mph, or just under 200 kilometers per hour. It was reputed to be the first Rolls-Royce designed to metric dimensions and the first in which the grille was angled for a more sporty look (a very slight angle, it must be said).

When launched in 1975 at just under £30,000 (ca. $84,000) in Britain, the Camargue was said to be the most expensive production car in the world. By 1986 the Camargue was still supposedly available on special order at something over £80,000. Takers were few.

At least the American magazine *Motor Trend* was positive, saying: "There are cars which will accelerate faster, there are some which will handle better; there are even one or two which, in specific circumstances, are even quieter. But in this writer's opinion, there are none which can rival the Carmargue's ability to transport its occupants in such splendid isolation." Most other journals were content to marvel at the "automatic air-conditioning system" that allowed the driver to select a chosen temperature. A complex network of sensors did their best to maintain the set choice; the unit would even give different temperatures for the upper and lower parts of the interior.

Amid that modest total of 534 Camargues was one Bentley-badged version, built for a customer who wanted to be doubly exclusive—and clearly wasn't too concerned about resale.

Jaguar XJ220

The Fattest Cat

In the late 1980s a vast number of people seemed to be in possession of a vast quantity of money. And by a quirk of financial history, this new wealth—apparently created out of nothing—had been distributed in perfectly inverse proportion to taste and restraint.

What better opportunity to launch the widest, ugliest, most ostentatious, altogether stupid Jaguar of all time?

From the moment this car—known as the XJ220—was shown in 1988, potential buyers were hammering on the showroom doors. Never mind that it was going to cost £415,554 (over $800,000) ex-factory, was so wide it wouldn't fit down many roads, so powerful it was totally impractical in traffic, and so highly strung it would need to be shipped back to headquarters regularly for obscenely expensive, racing car–style servicing. Within 48 hours of the announcement of "limited edition" production, 1,500 people had put up their hands for the 350 cars scheduled to be built.

These people either believed they needed one (they didn't) or that it would go up in value (it wouldn't). Those who got in first paid a 10 percent deposit, while others forked out even more to buy a spot in the queue. Behind this daft scenario, which was all to end in tears, there was a fair bit of cutting, chopping, and changing within the Coventry cathouse.

The original show car had featured a 6.2-liter V-12 and all-wheel drive. By the time specifications of the production version had been fixed, the XJ220 had a 3.5-liter V-6 (a later iteration of the engine fitted to the Metro 6R4 Rally car years before), and this powered only the rear wheels. Nonetheless, the production version boasted power and torque figures of 537 bhp (404 kW) and 474 lbs-ft (642 Nm), plus the ability to rocket from rest to 60 mph in under four seconds and to 95 mph in under eight seconds.

The XJ name was designed to bring to mind the XK120 model and the stillborn XJ13 racer. The "220" was the projected top speed in miles per hour (354 km/h), which would make the XJ220 the world's fastest production car. Except the real top speed came up at least 7 mph short—and the later, greater (but equally unsuccessful) McLaren F1 was soon to blow the Jaguar and other "world's fastest car" aspirants into the weeds.

The XJ220 was 7.3 feet wide, a fraction under 16.5 feet long, and weighed 3,234 pounds. Each of the four tires was unique (so there was no spare), and each tire cost about the same as a secondhand car. At the press launch a journalist from *The Guardian* grabbed the

wrong gear at high speed and, depending on whose report you believe, did thousands or tens of thousands' worth of damage. He wasn't the only one who had difficulty controlling this fearsomely quick, cumbersome, and harsh machine.

Autocar magazine said the engine sounded like "a pail of nuts and bolts being poured through a Magimix." In short, the XJ220 was not the sort of thing that the fashion designers and rock stars who had ordered it were even slightly likely to enjoy driving. Worse still, the production run didn't begin until July 1992, by which stage the economy had turned, the McLaren F1 had been unveiled, and so many buyers were so keen not to proceed they were willing to walk away from their substantial deposits. That wasn't good enough for Jaguar, which called in the lawyers to force completion. Many prospective buyers had already gone broke in the downturn, or simply refused to supply the balance, citing such things as the changed mechanical specifications. Settlements were reached, but it was a miserable business all around.

And how collectable was this so-called instant classic? A dozen or so years after the launch, a pristine example with low miles would struggle to fetch a quarter of the original price. And did anyone feel sorry for the fools who had bought them new? Not bloody likely.

Zil

No A to Z of bad cars can be complete without the fortuitously named Zil (although Yugoslavia's Zastava Yugo and the Ukraine's Zaz brand also do their best to bring up the rear end of the alphabet).

The Zil company commenced operation in Moscow in 1936 and for many years provided the cars of choice for Politburo members. The ludicrously large Zil 4104 and even more breathtakingly obese 41047 made it into the twenty-first century, each powered by a 7.7-liter V-8 and weighing 3.96 and 4.62 tons, respectively. Although the bent-eight was ancient and fed by carburetor, the maker claimed the rather impressive power and torque figures of 308.5 bhp (232 kW) and 449 lbs-ft (608 Nm).

Pictured here is a 1970 model, which a Tass news agency caption called a "light passenger car." Although it looked like pure Americana of the 1950s, by the mid-1980s Zil models had been heavily updated—to look more circa 1963 Dallas motorcade.

It appears that Zil production finally spluttered to a halt around 2003.

Fascination

Tomorrow's Car . . . Tomorrow

With radical wheel layout, a miracle engine, and styling so far ahead of its time that we're still not ready for it, the Fascination lived up to its name. Mind you, it could have equally lived up to several other names, including Hopeful, Ludicrous, and Daft.

It was in early 1973 that the Fascination was announced, with its American maker, the Highway Aircraft Corporation (HAC, a syndicate of American investors), calling it "Tomorrow's Car Today." It turned out to be more a case of tomorrow's car tomorrow, or perhaps the day after. Or never. Amazing claims were made in lavish brochures and full-page newspaper advertisements. The Fascination, readers were told, was "low cost, economical, safe, smog-free, modernistic, quiet, easy-to-handle and easy-to-park."

The vehicle was the brainchild of one Paul Lewis of Sidney, Nebraska. The "smog-free" claim was based on HAC's having an option on a "new, revolutionary, smog-free, boilerless steam engine" being developed by—stop me if you've heard this before—the Boilerless Steam Engine Corporation. While this power plant was being readied, the Fascination would be available with a 70 bhp (52 kW) Renault "four." Thanks to the "patented aerodynamic shape" this four-cylinder power plant would somehow enable the Fascination to achieve "100 mph and 40 mpg."

Showing a stronger grasp of hyperbole than practical car design, HAC claimed the Fascination was "the type of car millions of buyers want." Acceptance by the public would be "instantaneous because of the new and improved features and its perfectly streamlined beauty." The vehicle's unique front-wheel design (the technical spec sheets described the Fascination as using "single- or dual-

guide wheels"), would triple tire life. The vehicle would be so stable that overturning would be virtually impossible.

Highway Aircraft Corporation announced that production would start in the United States, then expand to other countries. By March 1973 HAC claimed to have signed up 36 American dealers, but, strangely, no production cars were delivered in that year—nor in any of the years that immediately followed.

Nevertheless, various people were still laboring to put the car on the road. One was a Los Angeles–based inventor, Edwin V. Gray, a man who claimed to have been working for over 20 years on what he called the Electro-Magnetic Association engine. Gray announced his power plant to the world in 1973, at the time of the first energy shock, the very moment when the Fascination people were finding that the world wasn't exactly beating a path to their door. Gray claimed his engine harnessed static electricity and thereby could answer all the world's power needs, with no fuel use and, thanks largely to its cool running, virtually no wear.

The Fascination people announced Gray's engine would replace their boilerless steam engine—not that they'd produced a boilerless steam engine or sold an actual car. Fascination press releases now headlined "$6 Million Fund Raised to Perfect the World's First No-Fuel Engine."

From there it descends into a standard conspiracy-theory story. Neither the Los Angeles County district attorney's office nor the Securities and Exchange Commission believed statements made in the prospectus. Raids were conducted and Gray claimed that during these raids all his drawings and prototypes were confiscated. "There has been a lot more to the suppression of my ideas than meets the eye," said Gray, not at all paranoid.

Hereafter, it gets a little harder to follow. A 1977 press release announced that a certain EBCO Inc. had entered into a contract with HAC to manufacture the "Fascination Space Age Transportation Innovation." By 1981, the same car was being referred to as the "Fascination by Spencer Industries." The only thing that remained constant was that you couldn't buy one. That said, at least one (presumably a Renault-powered prototype completed around 1974) actually did make it onto the road and is reportedly now in the hands of an American collector.

Lada 110

After punishing the Russian people and a few foreigners for more than a decade with the dire and distressing Lada Samara (also known as "the 1300," "the Volonte," and "the cause of the blockage"), the pioneers of Total Quality Mismanagement and Not-Quite-in-Time production supplemented it with an all-new model.

It was the Lada 110, launched in 1995. Lada claimed to have incorporated

design suggestions from Porsche into the 110. If so, they must have been along the lines of "Ve vould not do it like zat, if ve vere you."

To many car buyers, the sign of quality is a car with doors that shut with a resounding *clunk*. In keeping with the quality Lada buyers expected, the 110 had doors that opened with a resounding *clunk*.

Mazda Roadpacer AP

The Bloatary

It seems almost inconceivable today that a Japanese carmaker planning a new range-topping luxury car would turn to the Australian arm of General Motors for the body. But Mazda did exactly that in 1975, putting its logo loudly and proudly on a body built by Holden and renaming it the Roadpacer.

The Roadpacer was announced on April 1—a date that may or may not have any special symbolism in the Land of the Rising Sun—and was essentially an Australian-built Holden Premier frame loaded with "all the extras" and fitted with a Mazda 13B Wankel rotary engine.

The Roadpacer was intended only for the Japanese market. For three years annual reports pictured the car as "standing on top of the Mazda line-up of passenger cars," but the Roadpacer was a sales disaster. There were various factors at play. One was the still-lingering effect of the energy shock and the Wankel engine drank like a salaryman at the end of a long week.

The Roadpacer was also too wide, causing problems on typically narrow Japanese streets. More important, it attracted the special "wide-car tax." This was one of those curious and mysteriously changing levies the Japanese government used to ensure that the country's "open market" would remain almost completely free of imports.

On the plus side, the broad-in-the-beam Roadpacer had interior space that few other Japanese cars could match. Every gadget and gizmo in Mazda's armory was brought to battle. The Roadpacer had a central locking mechanism (borrowed from another model and accordingly ill-fitting) with an additional control that brought it automatically into play when the car reached the death-defying speed of 6 mph. There was also power steering, dual-zone air conditioning, and a car refrigerator.

Although top speed was claimed to be 95 mph, at 55 mph a loud musical tone sounded. This was presumably to remind Japanese drivers that they had an additional 40 mph up their sleeve. Other Mazda changes to the basic Holden included softening the suspension to the point that the chassis bottomed out regularly on anything approaching a rough road.

Why a Holden body was chosen for a sedan with a rotary engine is hard to say. The shape gave Mazda no advantages in weight distribution and few in packaging (although the Wankel engine is famed for its compactness, Mazda managed to fill the cavernous engine bay with plumbing and accessories). The Roadpacer's curb weight was a hefty 3,465 pounds and the 13B rotary's high-revving

130 bhp (98 kW) would have been better used in a lighter, more sporty car (as Mazda was soon to show).

With the Roadpacer, Mazda went to great expense producing a car that was no quicker than a standard six-cylinder Holden Premier, yet used a great deal more fuel in exchange for little more than additional smoothness.

And why did the Roadpacer die within three years? Using an imported body was a curious choice from day one, and many people at Mazda were always unhappy about their range-topping model being so obviously foreign. More important, the fuel crisis and the cost of developing the Wankel engine had bankrupted Mazda in the same way the Wankel had spelled the end for an independent NSU in Germany. Other Japanese companies were suffering to the point that Japan's department of industry, MITI, couldn't engineer the usual bailout or merger. Reluctantly, Mazda began negotiations with Ford, in search of much-needed capital.

Aside from the Roadpacer's dismal sales, a connection with General Motors no longer looked like a viable option, and the car was killed off a few months before Ford completed its purchase of 25 percent of Mazda's shares. If not for the success of the 1979 RX-7, Mazda's rotary-engine program would almost certainly have died as well.

AMC Pacer

Marketing textbooks define durable goods as consumer products that are typically used over an extended period and can survive repeated uses. The AMC Pacer was neither durable nor good.

What American Motors called "the first wide small car" appeared in mid-1975 and was grossly overweight, surprisingly tight on elbow room (despite possessing considerable girth), prone to cooking its occupants under that huge greenhouse, and diabolical in the handling stakes. Other than that, there weren't too many problems, except, of course, that it was shoddily screwed together and ugly. Really, really ugly. And if googly eyes and a ridiculously bulbous tail with a huge overhang over the side  of each rear wheel weren't enough, the Pacer was expensive to build and buy, and despite its so-called subcompact dimensions, it guzzled fuel.

The short hood was originally shaped for a GM-built Wankel engine. When this plan was stillborn, AMC engineers instead jammed in their hefty and well-aged six, making the Pacer as agile as an ocean liner and as desirable as gout.

Bugatti EB 110

Great Name, Lousy Arithmetic

I t seems extraordinary in light of today's "brand is king" mentality, that one of the greatest names in automotive history could have been allowed to languish for so many years. Yet from the late 1940s until the early 1990s, the famed Bugatti brand name and logo was seen only on a small number of old and spindly road and race cars that seemed to become more valuable with every year.

When the name came back, it was with a huge, and rather perplexing, extravagance. The man behind it was the Italian financier Romano Artioli, who bought the rights to the original logos and relaunched Bugatti with a continuation of the model designation system used by the French-Italian maestro Ettore Bugatti when he built some of the world's most capable sports and racing cars during the 1920s and 1930s.

The order of the day for the reborn brand was outrageous parties, money-no-object commemorative rallies, a *Vogue Living*–style new factory in Modena (with an air-conditioned production line!), major exhibits at world motor shows, and large-format, high-gloss brochures that looked as though they cost more than some small cars.

While Artioli set about trying to prove that his new all-wheel drive EB110 coupe (unveiled in September 1991) was a worthy

claimant to the title of "world's best supercar," many were still busy questioning where the money came from, or dividing the several million dollars spent on parties by the minuscule number of cars likely to be sold at the sort of stratospheric prices being mentioned.

The EB110's body was low and angular, and it made extensive use of carbon fiber. The car had Lamborghini-style pop-up doors and a midmounted 3.5-liter V-12 engine that had 60 valves and was boosted by four turbochargers. The output was quoted as a massive

545 horsepower (410 kW), the claimed 0-to-60 time was 3.6 seconds, and trials on a banked oval produced a "verified" top speed of 206 mph. The developers claimed that 240 mph would be soon achieved, but like many claims made for the new Bugatti, this one never quite bore scrutiny.

Handling was spectacularly good, but working against the Bugatti (aside from its ludicrous complexity and rushed development) was its weight, which, upward of 3,520 pounds, blunted the real 0-to-60 mph time to more like 4.5 seconds. An SS (supersport) version managed to cut the weight by 330 pounds, thanks to the use of even more alloy and carbon fiber and the deletion of all the luxury items. Publicity was gained when the Formula One star Michael Schumacher bought an EB110—and even more when he crashed it and blamed the inadequate brakes.

In 1993 an exquisite-looking retro saloon, called the EB112, was first shown. It was also four-wheel drive, but was powered by a 6-liter 12-cylinder engine.

Alas, the EB112 never made it into production. The end came in late 1994, after an estimated 154 examples of the EB110 had been built, and was brought about by various factors: There were now too many supercars on the market (including the McLaren F1, which was faster and generally judged to be better than the Bugatti). In addition, the world's economic bubble, which had fed the supercar boom in the first place, had well and truly burst. The numbers needed to underpin the new Bugatti venture never really added up.

The reborn company was rekilled, but when creditors leaped in for the feast they discovered that the most valuable thing, the right to use the name and logo, was owned by a separate Artioli-controlled company and was out of their grasp. The German VW conglomerate eventually ended up with the Bugatti name (along with Bentley and others) during the great brand realignment of the mid- to late nineties.

Mitsubishi HSR-VI

Between 1987 and 1997 Mitsubishi thought it necessary to build not one, not two, but six generations of its HSR concept car. Each was just that little bit sillier than the one before, reaching a peak, so to speak, with the HSR-VI.

This was an "automated driving mode" vehicle with clamshell doors that inexplicably opened directly into the path of anyone trying to enter or exit the vehicle.

Mitsubishi had variously used the HSR label to stand for High Speed Running, Human Science Research, High-Sophisticated Research and, from 1995, Harmonic Science Research. The HSR-VI possessed 1997's silliest feature: if you chose "driver-operated" mode rather than "automatic pilot," the roof section rose when the car was in motion. It was explained in the accompanying Mitsubishi press material that this mechanical—ahem—erection was designed to "express the pleasure of the driver when personally handling the car."

Honda S600

Cheap Shrill

First seen in Japan in 1964, the S600 sportster provided a superb example of how a large number of good ideas can be brought together and fused to create one very bad one.

It was the first Honda car to be exported in reasonable numbers and to some foreigners it seemed to be entirely in keeping with Japan's long tradition of miniaturization. Others, however, argued that rather than being a shrunken car the micro two-seater was actually an enlarged motorcycle. It had chain-drive, for goodness sake, and pistons the size of pinheads, which broke the sound barrier inside a matchbox-size engine that idled at 40,000 rpm.

Okay, there was an exaggeration or two in that past sentence. But the S600 did have chain drive. The tachometer was red-lined at a stunningly high 12,500 rpm. Because there was no form of rev lim-

iter, many owners saw the motor climb to 14,000 rpm and more—
a sight often followed by a loud noise, then silence.

Two versions were sold: a convertible and, later, a coupe. Problem one was that the Honda was fiendishly expensive to produce and
bore a price tag dangerously close to that of "proper" English roadsters such as the Austin-Healey Sprite, which had full-size engines.
The lack of a left-hand-drive version meant the S600 never officially
made it to the States; at the Australian launch there was a claim
that Honda would one day be "as big a name in cars as it is in

motorbikes." Surely not even the executive who mouthed the words believed it. Dealers who had enjoyed success with Honda bikes turned up their noses. Many sports-car aficionados laughed.

Highly strung is the phrase that comes to mind. The S600 had a four-cylinder, water-cooled, twin-overhead-camshaft engine with four carburetors. Screaming its 600 cc (36.5-cubic-inch) head off, this madly complex motor pushed out a feisty 57 bhp (43 kW), giving the S600 a claimed top speed of 87 mph. But, as one mechanic put it, "You could hear it wearing out." What Honda considered a mini-masterpiece was unable to hang on to its roller bearings, was prone to rid itself of its oil, and, thanks to its motorcycle-style drive arrangements, became a champion at tearing up differentials. The S600 also regularly burned out its distributor points and suffered a myriad of other mechanical ailments. And, not surprisingly, the average owner didn't follow the handbook's rather inconvenient suggestion that the engine be warmed up for five minutes at 3000 rpm before the car was driven.

The S600's rear-wheel-drive layout and four-wheel independent suspension helped ensure good handling. Though the brakes were drums all round, they worked extremely well with such a light package, and the fuel economy was excellent. Furthermore, the convertible version had a novel solution to wind noise: the shriek of the engine and chatter of the chains completely drowned it out.

A spate of early engine seizures in Australia prompted the local importers to do their own testing. They realized that they were lucky it was only a spate rather than, say, an entirety. Honda in Japan responded by sending out a team of eight technicians. Working in

white gloves, to the amusement of locals, they replaced the engine in every single S600 in the country. Such an extreme reaction and fanatical attention to detail was part of the reason Honda did indeed become as a big a name in cars as it was in motorcycles. But there was still a long way to go and more horrible automotive misjudgment in store.

In 1966 a far more conventional rendition of the same theme, the shaft-driven S800, hit the market. Things were starting to look up, mechanically, but the reputation established by the S600 was still a hurdle, and the S800 wasn't much cheaper to build. Honda turned its sights to economy cars instead.

Volvo 760 GLE

Thinking Inside the Square

Sweden's Volvo company went into the 1980s with a car from the 1960s. However, with the 1982 launch of the first totally new Volvo in more than 15 years, the company was promising a revolutionary car for the 1990s and beyond. That car, the 760 GLE, was intended as the bold and striking model that would distinguish Volvo from every other make and enable the brand to soar upmarket and take on BMW and Mercedes-Benz. In reality, the 760 GLE was a pug-ugly tank of a sedan that did the company damage from which it has, arguably, yet to recover.

The new-for-the-1980s Volvo was perhaps the boxiest car ever launched. There was scarcely a curved line to be found anywhere on it, and those cumbersome chrome moldings along its bodywork seemed to speak of an earlier, unloved era. Even on the inside, the square and bulky instrument panel of old had been redesigned—to make it even squarer and bulkier.

"It will look good," Rover's head stylist, Roy Axe, said of the 760, "once they take it out of the packing crate."

Volvo officials offered rejoinders such as "Not everyone wants to drive a jellybean on wheels," but it seemed that more people did want to do that than drive a Volvo 760. The irony was that in order to see what an outsider could do, Volvo had originally commissioned Italdesign to style the body. The directors looked at the rounded, thoroughly modern Italian proposition and rejected it in favor of the work of its own designers. D'oh!

At the time it launched the 760, the Swedish firm was bullish, having just finished its most successful year in history in which it sold over 300,000 cars and station wagons. The plan to move further upmarket and take on BMW and Mercedes was less to do with hubris than with the fact that the bottom end of the luxury market was being swamped with Japanese cars that were well made, generously equipped, and a lot cheaper than anything coming out of Sweden.

The 760 GLE had a longer wheelbase and a wider track than the 200 series it partially replaced. Technically, it was business as usual: front engine, rear drive. The slightly revolutionary auto trannie with push-button overdrive came from Japan. The standard engine was the 2.8-liter V-6, as used in the 264 model. There was a high luxury specification and, in the Volvo tradition, lots of practical features and safety equipment.

Volvo claimed that "the science of aerodynamics has played a major part in shaping the car's strikingly different body design." But the drag coefficient figure turned out to be 0.39, which equates roughly to that of a barn. Traveling sideways. Indeed, the drag coefficient was so decidedly unflash that when a wagon version was later produced, it cut through the air more efficiently than the sedan.

Phil Scott, an Australian motoring journalist, remarked in Sydney's *Sun-Herald*, "The square-rigged, upright, and heavily chrome-embellished Volvo flagship goes against every styling trend to emerge from Europe in the past few years." He said the engine was way behind BMW's efforts and many other aspects of the technology were equally undeserving of a gold star. In a heated point-for-point response from Sweden, Volvo stated: "[We] do not follow trends because they often turn out to be just trends. . . . The 760 GLE will absolutely not look as dated in a few years as some cars with rounded teardrop shapes introduced lately."

Despite this assertion, what followed over the next few years was a desperate attempt by Volvo to round off all the 760 edges and make the car look more like the "rounded teardrop shapes introduced lately." But the company always seemed one step behind.

Arna

Despite anything you may unkindly think, Arna was not the Roman god of poor panel fit or popped engine seals. It was an acronym of Alfa Romeo and Nissan Automotive and was the name given to a car that looked like a Nissan Pulsar with an Alfa grille. The year was 1983 and Alfa and Nissan each thought they had good reasons to jump in the sack and spawn this unique Japanese-Italian "thorough-hybrid."

The Arna gave Nissan access to Italy's largely closed car market, while the financially challenged Alfa gained financial assistance from the Far East plus metal you couldn't see through after six months. But the car itself, which promised to bring the best of both worlds, instead managed to combine Nissan's flair and road manners with Alfa's build quality and reliability.

The body panels—many of which were produced in Japan—were screwed together in Italy and the vehicle was fitted with an Alfa grille and a 1.2-liter version

of the Alfa boxer engine. The Arna had an English sister, too, the daftly named Nissan Cherry Europe, which also "benefited" from Alfa power.

So successful was the venture that Arna became a household name. The household in question was located next to the Arna plant in Pratola Serra near Avellino.

Messerschmitt

Postwar Crime

It's easy today to forget that immediately after World War II, Germany (or West Germany, as the productive part was then known) became the world's number one manufacturer of vehicles for poor people. And when you see some of them, you realize that there is plenty to forget.

After the war the old Autounion AG was re-formed in the western sector as Auto Union. Boosted by cheap German labor and well-honed engineering skills, it became one of the world's largest motorcycle manufacturers during the 1950s and also spat out eccentric little two-stroke DKW delivery vans and cars. Bavaria's BMW (Bayerische-Motoren-Werke) built something like 150,000 examples of the horrid Isetta bubble car. Prevented from continuing with aviation production, the famed war-plane builder Messerschmitt turned out tiny, narrow, and equally horrid bubble cars of its own.

For Messerschmitt, the switch to carmaker came about when the company took over the Fend company's three-wheeler minicar project. Messerschmitt, the maker of the ME-109 airplane and other hits, developed the design and, from 1953, produced a succession of models. The first was the KR-175.

With three wheels and two seats, one behind the other, the Messie "cabin scooter" was an almost exact blending of motor scooter and car. It was bigger than a bread-box, but not by much, and it was certainly a great deal noisier. Regularly the subject of well-deserved ridicule, the coffinlike Messie hit the market in most countries at about half the price of a basic family sedan. It was considerably cheaper

than just about anything else with more than two wheels. After Germany, it was most popular in the UK, particularly during the Suez crisis. Reasonable numbers also went to Australia and the States.

The big advantage of these minuscule vehicles (perhaps the only one) was that the alternative was invariably walking. The passenger sat with legs straddling the front seat and the maker's boast that the storage space behind the second seat could also accommodate a child seems more than a little frightening by today's standards.

The most successful model was the three-wheeler KR200, built from 1955. Later, the more powerful (that's "more powerful" rather than, say, "powerful") Tiger 500 arrived.

The KR200 had a two-stroke air-cooled, single-cylinder engine with a capacity of just 191 cc (11.6 cubic inches). The "big banger" Tiger model had a half-liter engine driving twin rear wheels through a four-speed transmission. The rear wheels were positioned so closely together that both the need for a differential and any stability advantages that might have otherwise been associated with having an extra wheel were eliminated.

The Messie cabin-scooter was claimed to have many big-car features. Unfortunately, one of them was shared with the Lightburn

Zeta: you needed to stop the engine and restart it to drive in reverse. On the plus side, the Messie certainly offered full weather protection and good all-round visibility thanks to the fighter plane–style curved canopy (which was also ideal for roasting the occupants in the summer). Production ceased in Germany in 1961. By then, rising prosperity and the much more modern and practical Mini-Minor had made such vehicles an anachronism.

Jensen-Healey

Not Even Nearly

For one brief shining moment it looked like salvation for the British sports-car industry: a new two-seater roadster with a modern body, a double-overhead-camshaft engine, and not just one famous name on the bodywork but two. It was the Jensen-Healey, and as an extra bonus in the brand department, its alloy engine was made by Lotus. There was only one small problem: the Jensen-Healey was one of the shoddiest cars ever built.

Its gestation began in 1967, when the much-loved Healey 3000 ceased production because it was unable to comply with the stricter U.S. safety and pollution laws. The British Motor Company declared that the MGC (a horror of a six-cylinder MGB) would be the 3000's successor, but Kjell Qvale, a millionaire California car dealer and Anglo-sports-car fanatic, wanted a more credible replacement. He wanted it so badly he bought out Jensen, the revered English

sports-car builder and coach maker that had produced the Healey 3000 bodies.

In 1970 Qvale made Donald Healey (of Austin-Healey fame) chairman of Jensen Motors Ltd. and himself president. The Jensen-Healey appeared two years later and the sheer joy of seeing an all-new ragtop in depressed early 1970s Britain made the press rave. It soon became obvious, however, that the car was underdeveloped and the build quality obscene.

The Jensen-Healey was a mongrel, and many of the borrowed components were not too flash to start with. The Vauxhall Viva steering assembly was prone to fail under the weight of its new obligations, and the Chrysler transmission, although modified, also struggled to cope. The engine was a 2-liter fed by big Dellorto carburetors, or Strombergs on some export versions. It put out a respectable 140 bhp (105 kW) and torque of 128 lbs-ft (173 Nm), though with levels of noise and unreliability that would become legendary.

How's this for stupid? Park an early J-H on a slope and the contents of the fuel tank would slip past the carburetors and into the sump. Other vices, often less exotic but equally unforgivable, were found in every area of the engine, and most defied continuous updates and running changes. Many things that should have been

kept inside the Jensen-Healey leaked out, while things that should have been kept outside leaked in. The fold-down roof was frustratingly complicated to operate and tended to lack that one feature we most expect in a roof: an ability to protect us from the elements.

The body was a monocoque (unitary construction type), which made Ye Olde Traditional English Rust even more of a problem. Water seemed to be able to find its way into the leg space and other parts via huge panel gaps, and many Jensen-Healeys were soon sagging in the middle. Reports also spread of camshafts seizing, water pumps failing, door locks falling into doors, and endless electrical peccadillos.

Of the 10,453 Jensen-Healeys built, 7,709 went to the United States. Also built were about 450 examples of a particularly ugly fixed-roof GT version. Production ceased in 1976, by which point Jensen was in receivership.

Nash Metropolitan

Cold Comfort

No other vehicle in history has managed as convincing an impersonation of a prostrate refrigerator on caster wheels as the Nash Metropolitan. Perhaps then, it's no surprise that this automobile came from the corporation that also built Kelvinator white-metal goods.

The Metropolitan's Toyland appearance would later make it a collectable, but the car completely failed to be popular in its day. This was despite intensive market research that appeared to show that such a vehicle was just what American motorists of the 1950s were waiting for.

In many people's minds it was all Austin's fault. This is grossly unfair. Yes, the Austin Motor Company did build the Metropolitan, and it did so at its Longbridge plant in England. But it built the car entirely under contract, and to a U.S. template. The styling was the work of an independent designer, William Flajole, who—I'm guessing here—hoped people would take the Metropolitan home because they felt sorry for it.

It was a lack of expertise in the small-car field, and of the right production facilities, that led to the Nash-Kelvinator group's outsourcing the manufacturing to the company considered the international leader in small cars at that time, Austin. And so, from early 1954, this most un-American of American vehicles arrived on U.S. shores direct from a British manufacturer. A two-door hardtop and a convertible were offered. Both were short, narrow, and top-heavy, with only a hint of wheel arches and a strange notch in each door, which, taking into account the refrigerator heritage, might have been modeled on a butter compartment.

The Metropolitan was generously equipped, but not particularly cheap, despite its modest size and the fact the British pound was then held in the same esteem as British dentistry. The body was of

a monocoque, or unitary, construction type. The spare tire was on the tail, then considered a European touch. There was a contrasting roof color, and eventually an elaborate two-tone paint job.

Under the hood

was Austin's tiny (by American standards) 1.2-liter four-cylinder A40 engine. The zero-to-60 mph sprint was more like a stroll. It took around 30 seconds. To market such a small, low-powered, curiously styled vehicle in the States in the 1950s was brave. An increasing number of American cars had twice as many cylinders and four times the engine capacity.

A second wind—okay, a gentle breeze—was provided in 1956 by a 1.5-liter Metropolitan with revised styling, improved equipment levels, and 25 percent more power. But sales numbers continued to be modest (to put it politely), and perhaps reached the level they did only because it was almost impossible to slake America's thirst for new cars in the 1950s.

Within a couple of months of the first Metropolitan going on sale, Nash had merged with Hudson to form American Motors Corporation, so some Hudson-brand Metropolitans were also sold before 1957, after which the new concern decided to concentrate on the Rambler brand. At this point the Nash and Hudson nameplates were dropped and the car became simply "the Metropolitan." It was also marketed under that simple moniker in the UK when Austin purchased the right to sell it in the home market. Or, more correctly, the right to fail to sell it in the home market.

The Metropolitan was finally hit on the head with a brick in 1961, though unsold stock kept showrooms full until well into 1962.

Nissan Pintara

A Bird? A Plane? No, Alas, a Superhatch

It was a decade that produced its fair share of Australian motoring horrors, but one car bestrides the harbor of 1980s failures like a colossus. It is the 1989 Nissan Pintara, which managed to be every bit as unsuccessful as the Leyland P76 without being even a tiny fraction as interesting. Indeed, when the Pintara petered out in an excruciatingly expensive meltdown of jobs, dollars, and egos, nobody even hinted that they were about to start an enthusiasts' club.

Where to start? During the 1980s Nissan Australia went berserk with its corporate checkbook, spending something like $500 million dollars upgrading its Clayton, Victoria, plant with the stated aim of producing 100,000 cars per year. What the company was going to do with all those cars was another question, but either no one asked, or someone had come up with a very persuasive way of saying it would all come right in the end.

Nissan Australia's then managing director was Ivan Deveson, something of a self-styled Lido "Lee" Iacocca (the extroverted Ford, then Chrysler, boss who wrote two large books—both about himself). With thumbs hooked into his trademark suspenders, Deveson described the new-generation Pintara as "Australian-designed" and boasted that it would be sold locally by Nissan and Ford (which would have its own Corsair version), and exported to places such as Japan "in large numbers." It wasn't.

The problems started when the Pintara was unveiled. It turned out to be merely a revamp of an already tired Japanese market front-drive "Bluebird" sedan. A locally adapted Pintara variant called Superhatch didn't help. More a hunchback than a hatchback, it was

as clumsy as the sedan was dull. It couldn't leap tall buildings and the speed of its sales brought to mind not so much a speeding bullet as a spent cartridge.

Scan the sales figures for the whole Pintara family: in 1990 just 13,688 Pintaras were sold (Mitsubishi Australia's Magna, which cleared over twice as many, 31,808, was considered to be struggling). In 1991 the Pintara body count was 11,819, then in 1992, just 5,569. And Nissan dealers had to "gut" (heavily discount) just about every one of them to achieve even these unimpressive figures. Ford did worse with its own Pintara, redubbed Corsair, selling 7,632, 3,562, and 1,891 cars during the same years.

It should be noted, however, that there have been plenty of cars worse than the Pintara—several of them made by Nissan. The Pintara was fairly well screwed together and had acceptable equipment levels, and even the 2-liter version offered competitive performance. But there wasn't a single compelling reason to choose one above the competition. And to achieve anything like its lofty ambitions, Nissan Australia needed more than a Superhatch. It needed a miracle machine.

By the end of 1992, local production of the Pintara/Corsair was finally killed off, and Nissan admitted to losses of hundreds of millions of dollars. And those high-volume Japanese exports? Only a thousand or so were shipped, each with a stuffed koala in the glove compartment and a badge saying "Nissan Aussie." The humiliation was complete.

Bricklin SV-1

No Winged Savior

A few years before John Z. De Lorean gave such a snappy image to sports-car failure, the Philadelphia-born Malcolm Bricklin demonstrated a similar level of automotive ineptitude with a remarkably similar car. Like the De Lorean DMC-12, the Bricklin SV-1 was an American-conceived, wedge-shaped, gull-wing-doored sports car with a body built from unusual materials.

Other parallels were equally curious: like the De Lorean, the Bricklin was produced outside the entrepreneur's native country with government backing from that country, was touted as a safety innovator, had woeful build quality, and lost millions. And it didn't stop there: some backers of the Bricklin fell for the old gull-wing sports-car trick a second time around and went on to put money behind De Lorean.

Malcolm Bricklin was a high-flying, fast-talking entrepreneur who started with a chain of Handyman hardware stores, then began importing motor scooters, before graduating to cars. He set up Subaru of America in 1968 but failed to make money out of it. That didn't stop him from trying to manufacture a car under his own name. To help the venture along, Bricklin did a deal with the Canadian province of New Brunswick, which would provide capital in return for jobs.

The Bricklin car, eventually unveiled in mid-1974, was powered by a Rambler 5.9-liter V-8. The acrylic and fiberglass body was supported by a heavy-perimeter chassis claimed (without much substantiation) to greatly improve occupant protection. The slant on

safety was largely because the car wasn't that quick. Anyway, a fuel crisis had struck since the car was first dreamed up, and a selfish sports car would be a hard sell. The quickly cobbled together slogan was "The Bricklin Safety Vehicle: You'll think it's ahead of its time. We think it's about time."

Even the gull-wing doors were heralded as a safety feature because "they opened out of the way of cyclists and pedestrians." This was sheer nonsense—they didn't even open out of the way of people trying to get in or out of the car. Malcolm Bricklin brashly announced that he had $100 million worth of advance orders. But the price tag was escalating from the original projection of $3,000 to a staggering $6,500 on release day and then on to nearly $10,000 six months later.

The Bricklin project was managed so haphazardly that the first batch of cars was shipped out of Canada incomplete. "Finishing kits" were later sent out, but these didn't cure leaking doors or a myriad of other problems. After a few months the Rambler V-8 was phased out, reputedly because bills had not been paid and the supply had been stopped, and a Ford unit was substituted.

Syndicated U.S. motoring correspondent Gero Hoscheck conducted an early road test. "The workmanship of the interior is quite miserable," he reported. "When I deposited my elbow on the armrest the whole door panel came off. I was horrified to find out the visibility was lousy. For a sports car and even by American standards the Bricklin has miserable brakes. . . . Active safety also seems inadequate for evasive maneuvres."

In *Car and Driver* (May 1975), Don Sherman wrote "Every [interior] furnishing seems to work against basic comfort. The roof is too low for headroom, the throttle pedal raises your right knee into interference with the leather steering-wheel rim and the lumpy seat doesn't offer support for your thighs. And it's a hard car to see out of as well."

It was hardly a surprise when, in October 1975, the gates to the Bricklin company were locked. Malcolm B was now saying he needed another Can$20 million to $25 million to keep the venture afloat. Not even New Brunswick officials (who had now spent Can$23 million, or five times the amount originally agreed) were that silly this time around.

Bricklin had originally said that his company would build 10,000 cars in the first year, that the number would rise to 50,000 by 1978, and that he had huge banks of advance orders. In reality, only 2,900 cars were built, and more than a third of them were unsold when the company shut its doors for good.

Biscuter

Despite its ultraexpensive adventure with the exotic Pegaso, Spain's Empresa Nacional de Autocamiones SA (ENASA) soon returned to car making. The second time around, the result was ultrainexpensive and just a little less than exotic.

The major push (words not chosen by chance) was behind a thing known as the Biscuter, which means "two-scooter." This tiny four-wheeled chariot of ire may have looked like it was styled by the Wiggles, but its origins actually rested with the French aeronautic pioneer Gabriel Voisin. He wanted to create a car even more basic than the Citroën 2CV, which itself came from a design brief famously stipulating "four deck chairs under an umbrella." Voisin could find no interest in France, so he sold Spain on the idea.

The Biscuter was powered (just) by a one-cylinder engine designed (badly) by Villiers and built (even badlier) by ENASA. The vehicle acquired the nickname Zapatilla, after the open slippers worn by peasants, and thanks to an almost complete lack of competition it became sus-

piciously close to popular. Production lasted from 1953 to 1960.

During a road test by the British magazine *The Motor*, a Biscuter broke down six times and recorded a fuel figure of 16 mpg, against a claim of "up to 63 mpg." The journalist at the wheel, Richard Bensted-Smith, wrote: "The greater part of the noise, smell, and confusion live with the engine between the front wheels, which drive and, God willing, stop the machine at the behest of the driver sitting with as many friends (up to one and a half) as he can persuade to accompany him roughly amidships." The magazine did not go on to recommend the Biscuter to readers.

Trabant P601

Workers' Triumph

The widely held belief that the bodywork of the East German Trabant was reinforced with cardboard was a vicious lie spread by antirevolutionary forces in the pay of capitalist roaders.

There was no cardboard in the body of the glorious people's car of the German Democratic Republic. To strengthen its Duraplast outer panels, the Trabant's makers used nothing less than genuine cotton fiber.

The Trabi—as it became commonly known—was much more than an automobile. It was a subject of derision, an environmental disaster, a danger to those inside and out, and an international declaration that Communism didn't work.

Ironically, the eastern parts of Germany had a fine tradition of car building. Before World War II, the Horch luxury brand, which was part of the Auto Union concern, was produced in the same Zwickau factories that later disgorged the Trabant. But unfortunately, when the East German workers seized control of the means of production from their exploiters after the war, automotive standards quickly slipped behind those of the running-dog capitalists on the other side of the divide.

The Trabi was the product of the Sachsenring company, which, after producing tractors and trucks during the late 1940s, turned to making cars based on prewar designs from the DKW company. These had front-mounted two-stroke engines and—by the mid-1950s— bodywork made from Duraplast. This cotton fiber–reinforced resin was cheaper and easier to come by than steel (which the military

had first dibs on anyway). And, unlike fiberglass, it could be shaped in a press and didn't need to be painted, as long as you were happy with a finish like that of a Bakelite radio.

Sachsenring's P70 model—unveiled amid government-approved levels of excitement at the 1955 Leipzig Industry Exhibition—captured the essential ingredients of the later Trabant; indeed a slightly smaller version produced from 1957, the P50, was the first vehicle to use the Trabant name.

The Trabant P50 represented carmaking at its most basic but could transport four adults in discomfort. It mutated into the P60; then in 1964 a major reskinning produced the longest-running and best-known Trabant, the P601 model.

The Trabant P601 was not a complete disaster from day one. There were economy cars on the other side of the divide that were very similar (the Goggomobil sedan, for example). But the likes of Goggomobil knew when to throw in the towel, which was very quickly. The Trabi P601, however, kept going for nearly 30 years and became internationally infamous when thousands of them noisily spluttered through the ruins of the Berlin Wall in 1989.

The P601 was powered by a 600 cc (36.5-cubic-inch) two-stroke twin, which was air-cooled for lower cost and higher noise. And the bodywork looked like a child's drawing of a Triumph Herald, itself several years old by 1964 and no masterpiece.

The Trabi P601 had a big door on each side that never looked properly closed, and silly little fins on the tail, even the station-wagon version. But what was it like to drive? Crap, actually. It was noisy, smoky, smelly, and badly built, with shocking brakes, dire performance, miserable handling, and a 6-volt electrical system so dismal you almost needed a torch to see if the headlights were on.

However, improvements were made in ensuing years, transforming the Trabi from a primitive, badly built Eastern European deathtrap into a primitive, badly built Eastern European deathtrap with a 12-volt electrical system.

In the late 1980s, glasnost and perestroika opened the door for an agreement to be reached for VW to supply 1.1-liter four-stroke Polo engines for an improved 1988 version of the P601. When Communism collapsed soon afterward, the two-stroke was phased out completely and only Polo-engined models were built. Not that anyone much wanted them; with the disappearance of restrictions on what car they could buy, people from the East could finally turn their backs on Duraplast and tail fins.

Despite the odiousness of the styling, mechanical attributes, and build quality, Trabants were exported in small numbers even to non-Communist countries from the 1960s. In the 1990s the car became positively trendy as a symbol of the old East. Working and non-working examples turned up as everything from highly decorated weekend runabouts to components of conceptual artworks. Production finally ground to a halt in 1991.

Scamp

During the 1960s and early 1970s it was generally agreed that if you were going to build an electric car, it had to be tiny, demonstrably unstable, and/or unspeakably ugly. Better still, all three.

Which brings us to the Scamp. This two-seater fiberglass-bodied micro is described in some circles as "the last car solely conceived, designed, and built in Scotland."

Don't be fooled by the Cyclops eye and trinket styling—these people were serious. They thought they could take on the Mini-Minor, the Hillman Minx, and other British small cars with an electric vehicle possessing just two seats, a miserable

range of 18 miles between charges, and a price that was dangerously close to that of a real car.

The Scamp was designed to keep Scottish Aviation engineers busy after production of the twin-engined Prestwick Pioneer airplane came to an end, circa 1964. Finance was provided by the Electricity Council, which intended to sell the Scamp next to washing machines and light fittings in its Main Street showrooms.

Stirling Moss, who was no stranger to touting British cars that had plenty of room for improvement, lent, or rented, some kind words, but it wasn't enough. The Scamp was absolutely flat out at 35 mph on the level, with one occupant. The old-fashioned lead-acid batteries—wired up to a salvaged airplane starter motor—were expensive to replace and needed recharging far too frequently.

Worse still, the Electricity Council insisted on independent safety evaluation by the Motor Industry Research Association. When the Scamp's suspension collapsed during the tests that followed, it made many people glad they weren't 16,000 feet up in something else made by Scottish Aviation. The rather spectacular failure also led to the Electricity Council's unplugging itself from the project.

Scottish Aviation continued for a while, but only 11 or 12 Scamps were made.